AMERICAN HISTORY

Environmentalism in America

Stephen Currie

LUCENT BOOKS
A part of Gale, Cengage Learning

GALE
CENGAGE Learning

Detroit • New York • San Francisco • New Haven, Conn • Waterville, Maine • London

GALE
CENGAGE Learning™

LIBRARY OF CONGRESS CATALOGING-IN-PUBLICATION DATA

Currie, Stephen, 1960-
  Environmentalism in America / by Stephen Currie.
      p. cm. -- (American history)
  Includes bibliographical references and index.
  ISBN 978-1-4205-0210-7 (hardcover)
  1. Environmentalism--United States--History--Juvenile literature. 2. Environmentalists--United States--History--Juvenile literature. 3. Environmental protection--United States--History--Juvenile literature. 4. United States--Environmental conditions--Juvenile literature. I. Title.
  GE197.C876 2010
  333.720973--dc22
                                                                2009042372

Lucent Books
27500 Drake Rd.
Farmington Hills, MI 48331

ISBN-13: 978-1-4205-0210-7
ISBN-10: 1-4205-0210-7

Printed in the United States of America
1 2 3 4 5 6 7 14 13 12 11 10

Printed by Bang Printing, Brainerd, MN, 1st Ptg., 04/2010

Contents

Foreword

The United States has existed as a nation for just over 200 years. By comparison, Rome existed as a nation-state for more than 1,000 years. Out of a few struggling British colonies, the United States developed relatively quickly into a world power whose policy decisions and culture have great influence on the world stage. What events and aspirations drove this young American nation to such great heights in such a short period of time? The answer lies in a close study of its varied and unique history. As James Baldwin once remarked, "American history is longer, larger, more various, more beautiful, and more terrible than anything anyone has ever said about it."

The basic facts of United States history—names, dates, places, battles, treaties, speeches, and acts of Congress—fill countless textbooks. These facts, though essential to a thorough understanding of world events, are rarely compelling for students. More compelling are the stories in history, the experience of history.

Titles in this series explore the history of the country and the experiences of Americans. What influences led the colonists to risk everything and break from Britain? Who was the driving force behind the Constitution? Which factors led thousands of people to leave their homelands and settle in the United States? Questions like these do not have simple answers; by discussing them, however, we can view the past as a more real, interesting, and accessible place.

Students will find excellent tools for research and investigation in every title. Lucent Books' American History series provides not only facts, but also the analysis and context necessary for insightful critical thinking about history and about current events. Fully cited quotations from historical figures, eyewitnesses, letters, speeches, and writings bring vibrancy and authority to the text. Annotated bibliographies allow students to evaluate and locate sources for further investigation. Sidebars highlight important and interesting figures, events, or related primary source excerpts. Timelines, maps, and full-color images add another dimension of accessibility to the stories being told.

It has been said the past has a history of repeating itself, for good and ill. In these pages, students will learn a bit about both and, perhaps, better understand their own place in this world.

1607
The first permanent British colony in North America is founded in Jamestown, Virginia.

1743
Thomas Jefferson is born.

1789
The U.S. Constitution goes into effect.

1803
Meriwether Lewis and William Clark lead an expedition from Missouri to the Pacific Coast.

1600	1625	1650	1675	1700	1725	1750	1775	1800	1825

1848
Karl Marx and Friedrich Engels publish *The Communist Manifesto*.

1861
The U.S. Civil War begins.

1872
Yellowstone is set aside as a wilderness park.

1869
First east-west railroad across the United States is completed.

1914
World War I begins.

American Environmentalism

1929
The Great Depression begins.

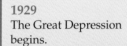

1954
The U.S. Supreme Court rules against segregation in schools in *Brown v. Board of Education*.

1948
Smog in Donora, Pennsylvania, kills several people and sickens many more.

1850	1875	1900	1925	1950	1975	2000	2010

1997
The Kyoto Protocol is proposed.

2001
Terrorists hijack four airplanes, destroying the towers of the World Trade Center and damaging the Pentagon.

1962
Rachel Carson publishes *Silent Spring*.

1970
Congress passes the Clean Air Act Extension; the first Earth Day celebration is held.

America and the Environment

In a modern, urban society such as the United States of the early twenty-first century, the link between human beings and the natural world often seems fragile. Many Americans can go for days only dimly aware of their environment—that is, the wildlife, landforms, and climate surrounding them. Air-conditioning and central heating allow millions of people to control the temperatures of their homes and workplaces. Advances in telecommunications permit an ever-growing number of Americans to work, shop, and socialize without setting foot in the outdoors. Moreover, many commentators believe that Americans are less and less interested in the land and outdoor activities. "Nature is more abstraction than reality," writes author Richard Louv. "Increasingly, nature is something to watch, to consume, to wear—to ignore."[1]

This generalization does not apply to everyone. Plenty of twenty-first-century Americans enjoy outdoor activities ranging from gardening to hiking. Similarly, landscapers, ski instructors, and construction workers are among many whose jobs take them outside. Still, from indoor pools to enclosed malls, American society is moving away from the outdoor world—and setting itself more and more apart from nature. On hot summer days, as present-day Americans drive air-conditioned cars from their air-conditioned homes to their air-conditioned offices, they can almost forget that the natural world exists.

The truth, of course, is that human beings are connected to nature in thousands of ways. The actions of people affect the animals and plants around them and can have a major impact on the physical world of rivers, hillsides, and canyons as well. In turn, what happens in nature affects the well-being of humanity. The connections are so strong that ecologists, or scientists who study how elements of nature interact, usually consider human beings to be a vital part of the environment. In their view, people are not separate from the natural world. Instead, they are simply one aspect of it, and their fate is tied to the fate of the environment around them.

The fate of the environment, though, has not always been a concern for political leaders and the American public. Throughout history, Americans have damaged the environment as often as not. Factory owners have dumped waste into waterways, making them uninhabitable for birds and fish and sometimes contaminating the water supply for people. In a never-ending search for fuel, coal mining companies have turned wooded mountaintops into barren, muddy craters. Americans have hunted animals nearly to extinction, built roads through environmentally sensitive wetlands, and sprayed toxic chemicals across farm fields and suburban lawns alike. The history of the United States in many ways is the story of environmental damage, much of it done with little if any thought about the impact on nature and on humans themselves.

Not all Americans have agreed with this way of thinking. Over the years many scientists, writers, and political leaders have feared that human activity is harming the environment—and by extension, humanity. These men and women have advocated new laws and policies designed to protect and replenish nature; they have worked, moreover, to change the way people think about the world around them. Today we call these thinkers environmentalists and the perspective they advocate environmentalism. Perhaps the best summation of the environmentalist philosophy comes from the work of Aldo Leopold, a Wisconsin naturalist best known for his 1949 book *A Sand County Almanac*. "A thing is right," Leopold wrote, "when it tends to preserve the integrity, stability, and beauty of the biotic community [the natural world]. It is wrong when it tends otherwise."[2] Over the years environmentalists have waged many battles to "preserve the integrity, stability, and beauty" of the environment—or, as Leopold might have put it, to do, quite simply, what is right.

Success and Failure

The record of the environmental movement has been mixed. At times it has been highly successful. In the late 1800s and early 1900s, for example, political leaders shielded some of the country's most beautiful landscapes from development, preserving as wilderness regions such as Yellowstone in Wyoming and Yosemite in California. Later, the work of environmentalists in the 1960s and 1970s led to laws that limited pollution, protected endangered animals and plants, and banned the use of certain chemicals. The successes of the environmental movement are easy to find today as well. Communities from coast to coast offer recycling programs, advertisements trumpet the eco-friendliness of products, and the populations of once-vanishing animal species such as the American bison and the bald eagle are on the upswing.

A photograph depicts a bald eagle in flight. The environmental movement helped raise the population of the bald eagle species, which was once on the edge of extinction.

It would be wrong, though, to view the environmental movement as an unbroken series of successes. Over the years the movement has had its share of failures. The activists of the late 1800s could not save some of the most ecologically sensitive lands of the American West from being flooded or leveled to suit human purposes. Environmental awareness came along too late for the passenger pigeon, which became extinct in the early 1900s. Groundbreaking as the antipollu-

tion laws of the 1970s were, some of the gains they made were reversed by later presidential administrations. The effectiveness of the movement, then, has been by no means steady.

Nor would environmentalists today claim that the battle has been won. On the contrary, many activists worry that the dangers faced by the environment in the early twenty-first century are more significant than ever. The United States has been unable to reduce its heavy consumption of oil, coal, and natural gas, energy sources that cause pollution and contribute to climate change. Each year developers convert hundreds of square miles of forests, marshes, and fields into buildings, roads, and parking lots, degrading the land and destroying habitat. And the unwise environmental decisions of previous generations resound today, whether in the form of toxic substances left in the ground by the manufacturing processes of an earlier time or in the form of policies favoring cars over public transportation and the use of oil and coal over energy sources such as the sun and the wind.

Despite the setbacks, though, the environmental movement remains strong. Environmentalists of today regularly weigh in on many important political debates, from the battle over global warming to the questions surrounding national energy policy. Environmental organizations such as the Sierra Club are powerful voices in support of the welfare of the planet. Many factors have contributed to the continued importance of environmentalism today, among them concepts of justice and fairness, lessons from scientific research, and the voices of Americans as disparate as nineteenth-century activist John Muir, twentieth-century scientist Rachel Carson, and former vice president Al Gore. The work of earlier environmentalists, the successes of earlier environmental battles, and the hope of a brighter, more ecologically friendly future—all of these provide inspiration and energy to the environmental activists of our time.

Chapter One

The Roots of Environmentalism

Many Americans see environmentalism as a relatively recent movement. This perspective makes some sense. The laws of today that protect the natural world generally date back only to the 1960s and 1970s, and concerted efforts to educate the public about environmental issues began at about the same time. Indeed, the word *environmentalism* was not used in its current meaning until about 1966; before that the word referred instead to a theory about human development. And those who argue for a starting point before the 1960s typically look no further than the late 1800s, when for the first time Americans began protecting wilderness areas for future generations.

However, the environmentalist movement did not spring full-fledged into existence during the late 1800s, let alone the middle of the twentieth century. In fact, the roots of the movement lie further back in American history. The successes

environmentalists achieved in the 1880s and the 1960s owe much to the ideas of earlier American thinkers and leaders. Throughout its history, the environmental movement has drawn on themes of religion, ethics, science, law, and economics—themes that run deep in American thought among naturalists, philosophers, and even artists. Well before the first national park was established, well before the passage of antipollution legislation, the forces that would eventually result in these events were already at work.

Nature and Colonization

The history of the modern United States began with the colonization of North America's Atlantic coastline by the British. The first permanent English colony was established in 1607 in Jamestown, Virginia. Other colonies soon followed: Massachusetts, Maryland, South Carolina. Through the mid-1700s the colonies grew steadily as a stream of arrivals from England, Germany, and other western European nations also crossed the ocean to settle in America. These new arrivals brought with them their culture, their values, and their ways of thinking about the world. These ways, naturally enough, became the ways of the colonists—and the ways of America.

One of the most deeply held European ideals during the period of colonization had to do with the environment. For western Europeans of the time, the natural world existed for one reason only: to meet the needs of human beings. When Europeans needed firewood or timber, for example, they simply cut down the trees they needed—without regard to the potential impact on the environment. In the same way, the residents of European towns and cities found it convenient to dispose of their garbage by dumping it into rivers and lakes—and so they did exactly that, with scant concern for what effect this would have on fish, waterfowl, or communities farther downstream.

Part of the reason for this way of thinking was the reality of life in Europe. Most Europeans of the time were farmers who were usually one bad harvest away from starvation. They did not have the luxury of protecting the environment at the expense of their own well-being. Few Europeans of the 1600s would have stopped hunting pheasants, say, simply because it seemed that the number of pheasants was dropping, or would have walked twice as far as necessary to collect firewood, just because going farther allowed them to gather the wood in an environmentally

sensitive manner. As naturalist Aldo Leopold put it in 1949, "Wild things . . . had little human value until mechanization assured us of a good breakfast"[3]— that is, until people no longer needed to worry about day-to-day survival.

Religion played a part in Europeans' anti-environmentalist perspective, too. According to the Bible, the natural world was made for the use of humans. "Fill the earth and conquer it," God commands in Genesis, the opening book of the Hebrew Bible or Old Testament. "Be masters of the fish of the sea, the birds of

A farmer and his son plow the fields. The colonists disregarded the conservation of nature and only viewed the surrounding environment as a way to meet their basic needs.

heaven and all living animals on the earth." (Genesis 1:28) Not just animals but plants, too, were placed under the control of people: "I give you all the seed-bearing plants that are upon the whole earth," God decrees, "and all the trees with seed-bearing fruit; this shall be your food." (Genesis 1:29) Other biblical passages, particularly in the Hebrew Bible, echo the theme that people are to be in charge of the living things around them.

Whatever the cause, however, the European view of nature had little real effect on the European environment during the 1600s and early 1700s. Technology was not well developed, which limited human impact on the world. Farmers, for example, worked their land with plows and hoes rather than with mechanical combines. Low population

figures played a role, too: The population was too small to make major changes to the earth. True, the world was not pristine. The Thames River, which runs through London, was polluted by household and municipal garbage along with human and animal waste, and in much of Europe fires for cooking and heating had covered churches and houses with a layer of soot. For the most part, though, the lack of people and the primitive technology kept the environment in generally good condition.

Natural Resources

Like their counterparts who remained in Europe, the first European colonists in North America did not hesitate to make use of their new homeland's wildlife, minerals, and landforms. Indeed, most

Settlers plant crops in South Carolina. Colonists made use of the fertile North American soil by farming a variety of crops.

of the early settlers were drawn to America in search of these natural resources. During the 1500s, for example, a number of Spanish explorers and colonists crisscrossed the Southwest in search of gold. Gold was also the attraction for the Englishmen who founded Jamestown, Virginia, in 1607. "There was no talke, no hope, nor worke," reported one of Jamestown's colonists, "but dig gold, wash gold, refine gold."[4] The colonists were extremely disappointed when they discovered that what they believed to be gold was actually iron pyrite, another mineral entirely.

As a result, when European colonists described the countryside of North America, they typically emphasized the economic value of the land. Many early writers focused on the continent's agricultural potential. "There is so much hay ground in the country [that] the richest voyagers that shall venture thither need not fear want of fodder, though his herd increase into thousands,"[5] wrote William Wood about New England in 1634. Settlers rhapsodized about the fertility of the soil and the variety of crops that could be planted in North America. One settler claimed that his crop of peas had grown 10 inches (25 cm) in just ten days. Others asserted that farming anywhere in America was easier and more productive than farming in even the most fertile parts of Europe.

Colonists also spoke enthusiastically about the value of American wildlife. Beavers were plentiful, for example, and their skins could be sold for high prices to meet the European demand for fur

hats. Whales were hunted for their bones, which could be turned into tools and other objects, as well as for their blubber, an important source of oil. Even the Pilgrims of Massachusetts, whose move to the New World was much less about economics than about politics and religion, noted the value of America's whales. "Large whales of the best kind for oil and bone came daily alongside and played about the ship,"[6] one observer reported as the Pilgrims drew near Massachusetts in 1620.

America's mineral resources, however, were what most captivated the explorers and the new settlers. Gold was a particular attraction, as it was the most valuable of all precious metals. Still, the prospect of finding other minerals enthralled Europeans as well. "We saw a very good piece of ground," reported Robert Juet, who sailed up New York's Hudson River in 1609, "and hard by it there was a Cliffe, that looked . . . as though it were either Copper, or Silver myne [that is, silver]; and I thinke it to be one of them, by the Trees that grow upon it."[7] In the end most of these deposits of copper, silver, and other materials proved no more real than the gold at Jamestown. Still, early European visitors were drawn to North America in hopes of finding—and using—these natural resources.

As for aspects of nature that had no obvious economic value, the early colonists typically tried to destroy them. Wolves, for example, roamed much of eastern North America when Europeans arrived, but they had been wiped out in

De Tocqueville on America and the Environment

Alexis de Tocqueville was a French aristocrat who had a deep interest in politics, government, and culture. In the early 1830s he traveled through parts of the United States to study the politics and customs of Americans. His findings appeared in two long publications, collectively known as Democracy in America. *De Tocqueville's work is still read today.*

While de Tocqueville's main concern was how democratic principles of government expressed themselves in American life, he wrote on other topics as well. Among these was the American view of the environment, which he saw as being several decades behind the thinkers of Europe:

Europe is much concerned with the American wilderness, but Americans themselves hardly give it a thought. The wonders of inanimate nature [that is, rocks, mountains, and other nonliving things] leave them cold, and it is hardly an exaggeration to say that they do not see the admirable forests that surround them until the trees fall to their axes. Another spectacle fills their eyes. The American people see themselves tramping through wilds, draining swamps, diverting rivers, populating solitudes [settling in quiet places], and taming nature.

Alexis de Tocqueville, *Democracy in America*, trans. Arthur Goldhammer. 1840. Reprint, New York: Library of America, 2004, p. 557.

A painting depicts Alexis de Tocqueville, a French writer who examined the American view of the environment.

most of this territory by the early 1800s. Wolves were threats to livestock, and colonists shot or trapped them to eliminate the danger. The fact that wolves helped keep rodent pests in check did not matter to most of the settlers. The natural world existed for the benefit of humans, and wolves, the settlers believed, harmed farmers more than they helped them. The wolves, then, had to go.

Science and Art

To be sure, early writers sometimes did appreciate American scenery and wildlife for its own sake. "The Land is very pleasant and high,"[8] noted Juet of a region near the mouth of the Hudson River. Others were intrigued by the dozens of birds and mammals of the New World, many of which were unknown in Europe, and wanted to learn everything they could about these animals and their habits. "Pliny and Isadore," reported colonist John Josselyn, referring to two famous authors of ancient Rome, "write there are not above 144 kinds of Fishes, but to my knowledge there are nearer 300." Josselyn proceeded to catalog all the fish species he knew about, many known only in the New World, and concluded by observing wryly, "I suppose America was not known to Pliny and Isadore."[9]

Over time, too, scientific interest in the

A drawing by John James Audubon depicts a group of blue jays feeding. Audubon and other artists helped Americans to see the beauty of the environment and wildlife.

natural world increased. One of the colonies' first naturalists was a Philadelphian named John Bartram. Born in 1699, Bartram was particularly interested in botany, or the study of plants. He traveled frequently into the American wilderness to collect seeds, flowers, and bulbs, and he corresponded regularly with naturalists in Europe. Though better known today for his work in politics and government, Thomas Jefferson was a gifted naturalist as well. His writings include detailed descriptions of waterfalls in the mountains near his Virginia home, studies of the impact of the weather on plant life, and much more. While Jefferson paid attention to the economic value of nature—he spent hours trying to develop hardier vegetables, for example—he was also deeply interested in the natural world for its own sake.

The connection between art and nature grew increasingly strong as well. John James Audubon was the most successful of many artists who primarily painted scenes from nature. Born in 1785, Audubon is best known for his colorful depictions of birds in their natural habitats. An avid outdoorsman, Audubon was never happier than when he was near birds and other animals. "Perhaps not an hour of leisure was spent elsewhere than in woods and fields," he wrote of his childhood. "To examine the eggs, nest, young, or parents of any species of birds constituted my delight."[10] His paintings were highly prized by naturalists and art collectors alike, and they helped open Americans' eyes to the beauty that could be found in American forests, rivers, and fields.

Writers, too, became more and more eloquent about the wonders of nature.

Religion, Culture, and the Environment

The traditional Judeo-Christian disregard for nature is not shared by all cultures. Many societies, now and in the past, have adhered to a religious view known as animism, in which holds that divine spirits are found all through the natural world. Animism was common among Native American cultures, for example. The pre-Christian societies of Europe were often animistic, too. "Before one cut a tree, mined a mountain, or dammed a brook," writes historian Lynn White Jr. about pre-Christian Europeans, "it was important to placate the spirit in charge of that particular situation."

It would be an exaggeration, however, to say that animistic societies live in total harmony with nature. On the contrary, animistic peoples have often caused devastation to the natural world. The Plains Indians used to drive whole herds of buffalo over cliffs, killing dozens more than they could use. The inhabitants of Easter Island in the Pacific cut down all the forests that originally covered the land. And the moa, a large, flightless bird of New Zealand, is just one of a number of animals that has died out due to overhunting. No culture or religion has a monopoly on poor environmental practice.

Lynn White Jr., "The Historical Roots of Our Ecological Crisis," Earth Talk Today. www.earthtalktoday .tv/earthtalk-voices/historical-roots-ecological-crisis.html.

John Bartram's son William, a naturalist like his father, wrote a popular book describing his travels in the South. While the book contained plenty of important scientific information, it also presented a romanticized view of the natural world, one in which animals were frequently given human motives and actions. "The laughing coots [waterbirds] with wings half spread were . . . hiding themselves in the tufts of grass," Bartram wrote of a lagoon in Florida. "Young broods of [birds] . . . following the watchful parent unconscious of danger, were frequently surprised by the voracious trout; and he, in turn, by the subtle greedy alligator."[11]

Jefferson and Catlin

Despite their interest in the natural world, most of these thinkers and artists saw no reason to protect or preserve nature. Indeed, their actions often harmed wildlife and the wilderness. Audubon, for example, did not use living birds as models for his famous paintings. Instead, he shot the specimens he wanted to paint and then arranged the dead birds against a suitable background. Worse, as a biographer notes, "The rarer the bird, the more eagerly [Audubon] pursued it, never apparently worrying that by killing it he might hasten the extinction of his kind."[12] The Bartrams, similarly, did not hesitate to uproot plants for further study.

Still, in the years following the American Revolution, several Americans did begin to show a concern for preserving the environment. One of the earliest of these Americans was Thomas Jefferson.

Many of Jefferson's lands were hilly and rocky, and one piece of his property contained a so-called natural bridge—an unusual rock formation in the shape of an arch. Jefferson called the bridge "the most sublime of Nature's works," and, though he was chronically short of funds, refused all offers from those who wished to buy the property. He feared that a buyer might destroy or otherwise disturb the formation. "I have no idea of selling the land," he wrote in 1815. "I view it in some degree as a public trust, and would on no consideration permit the bridge to be injured, defaced or masked from public view."[13]

Jefferson's concerns were echoed some years later, though more globally, by an artist named George Catlin. Catlin is best known today for paintings he made of Native Americans of the Great Plains, paintings he created primarily during the 1830s while living with several Indian groups. Catlin became deeply concerned about the survival of Indian culture as European settlers moved farther west. At the same time, he worried about the fate of the American bison, or buffalo. The settlers were killing as many buffalo as they could—sometimes for meat, but often only for their skins and occasionally merely for sport. This slaughter disgusted Catlin. The buffaloes were dying, he charged, so that white people could be "enveloped in buffalo robes"—a status symbol of the time—"and [wear] them ostentatiously amidst the busy throng [crowds]."[14]

Looking ahead, Catlin predicted disaster for the buffalo. Though millions of

these animals still roamed the Great Plains as late as 1840, Catlin expected that they would quickly die out as settlers moved ever west. Few Americans of the time thought much about extinction; Catlin was one of the few. The buffalo, he warned, was "rapidly wasting from the world. . . . Its species is soon to be extinguished."[15] In his eyes there was only one way to prevent the extinction of the buffalo. The federal government, he argued, should prevent whites from settling in much of the Great Plains, reserving that region for the Indians and the animals. "What a beautiful and thrilling specimen for America to preserve . . . !" he wrote enthusiastically. "A *nation's Park*, containing man and beast,

A painting by George Catlin depicts a bison hunt. Catlin was concerned for the buffalo species because the settlers frequently hunted bison for sport.

in all the wild and freshness of their nature's beauty!"[16]

Thoreau

Jefferson's focus was a specific rock formation, Catlin's the survival of a species.

Another American thinker of the 1840s, Henry David Thoreau, took an even broader view of nature and its relationship to humanity. A Massachusetts native, Thoreau was as careful an observer of the natural world as any American of

A portrait depicts writer Henry David Thoreau. Thoreau feared the impact urbanization would have on the surrounding environment.

his time. He was also a social critic who viewed the increasing urbanization of New England with alarm. Many of his writings urge Americans to pay more attention to nature—and to consider the effects of their actions on the world around them. To Thoreau, a world disassociated from wilderness was a world scarcely worth living in. Noting that human activity in New England had wiped out or severely reduced the numbers of wolves, bears, panthers, and other large mammals, for example, Thoreau wrote, "I cannot but feel as if I lived in a tamed, and, as it were, emasculated country."[17]

Thoreau's perspective on land ownership was even more radical. Thomas Jefferson had called the natural bridge on his property a "public trust."[18] In other words, it did not belong specifically to Jefferson, but rather to all Americans, and Jefferson had no right to damage or alter it. Thoreau took this notion even further. In his opinion most of nature should be viewed in the same way. Certainly, Thoreau argued, the most striking features of the natural world should not be in private hands. "If here is the largest boulder in the country," he wrote, "then it should not belong to an individual nor be made into door-steps. . . . Precious objects of great natural beauty should belong to the public."[19]

Finally, Thoreau was almost alone among Americans of his time in arguing that nature had a right to exist. Even Jefferson and Catlin were motivated to protect nature in part for the sake of people. Jefferson wanted Americans to enjoy looking at his natural bridge; Catlin hoped that future visitors to the Great Plains could see buffalo in their native habitat. Thoreau, who was never especially fond of people to begin with, argued from a different perspective. In his estimation nature took precedence over human beings.

"Monadnoc"

Mount Monadnock in southern New Hampshire stands considerably higher than any other nearby peak, making it a distinctive feature of the surrounding countryside. Monadnock was one of Henry David Thoreau's favorite places, and a number of other literary figures of Thoreau's time visited the mountain as well. Some, though not all, climbed to the 3,165-foot-high summit (965 m).

Many of these writers saw Monadnock as a mystical and inspiring place, an example of the power and beauty of the natural world. Thoreau certainly thought this way. So did Thoreau's friend Ralph Waldo Emerson, who in 1846 wrote a dense and extremely long poem called "Monadnoc" [the spelling used at the time], as did William Peabody, a little-remembered poet and minister whose verse, also called "Monadnoc," begins this way:

"Upon the far-off mountain's brow
The angry storm has ceased to beat
And broken clouds are gathering now
In lowly reverence around his [that is,
    the mountain's] feet."

William Peabody, "Monadnoc," Mount Monadnock. www.monadnockmountain.com/Monadnoc%20Peabody.htm.

A picture displays Mount Monadnock in New Hampshire during the fall. Through its natural beauty, the mountain inspired Thoreau and many other writers.

The natural world, he argued, was not simply a resource. Rather, it had an independent existence, and as such it was worthy of respect. "The earth I tread on," Thoreau wrote in 1851, "is not a dead inert mass. It is a body—has a spirit—is organic. . . . The solid globe," he concluded, "is the most living of creatures."[20]

George Perkins Marsh

Thoreau is widely considered an important influence on the environmentalists of the twentieth century, and many people think of him as the "father of the environmental movement,"[21] according to the Thoreau Farm Trust Web site. Within his own time, however, Thoreau was not the best-known American advocate for the natural world. This honor went, instead, to a man named George Perkins Marsh. Born in Vermont in 1801, Marsh had a long and varied career in academia, government, and law. He is best remembered, though, for his work on behalf of nature and the environment.

Unlike Thoreau, who had the soul of a poet, Marsh was a scientist at heart. An enthusiastic traveler and a careful observer, Marsh studied the natural world wherever he went. He was particularly interested in the effects that people had on the environment. At the time most Americans believed that any damage humans caused the earth was minor and easy to fix. Marsh's investigations, however, convinced him otherwise. Again and again he saw native plants and animals disappearing as people converted fields and forests to farms; over and over he saw human intervention throwing the

natural world out of balance. "Man is everywhere a disturbing agent," he wrote in 1864. "Wherever he plants his foot, the harmonies of nature are turned to discords."[22]

Marsh's studies suggested that changes brought about by humans had unexpected—and usually unwanted—effects. While visiting Greece, for example, Marsh noted that residents were rapidly clearing away forests to make room for more farmland. By studying weather records, Marsh discovered that the removal of the forests was connected to climate change. The lack of trees was apparently making the region hotter and drier, which in turn made it harder to grow crops. Similarly, when people killed birds and other animals that preyed on insect pests, Marsh noticed that the insect populations usually rose to alarming levels. He concluded that the killing of the predators was benefitting the pests, and warned people to think about possible consequences before acting.

In 1864 Marsh published his best-known book, an environmental text that he called *Man and Nature*. The book was surprisingly modern in its insights. Marsh demonstrated to a skeptical readership that all aspects of the natural world were deeply interconnected. He also emphasized the degree to which humans affected their environment—usually for the worse. In his writing Marsh advocated that Americans treat the earth with care and respect—partly to preserve the health of the natural world for its own sake, but also to avoid impacting nature in ways that would hurt human beings. Overall, Marsh's message was designed to make Americans think. "[His] insight that humans could do profound damage to the natural world was novel and startling,"[23] one commentator notes. Never before had anyone, scientist or poet, argued for nature in quite this way.

The ideas of men like Jefferson, Catlin, Thoreau, and Marsh were indeed new and thought provoking. At the time, though, they had relatively little influence on the way most Americans lived their lives. Where nature was concerned, Americans still tended to take from the land whatever they could get—and to ignore the consequences for the world around them. For every Thoreau who found natural beauty in the forests, rivers, and meadows near their homes, many more Americans saw nature as an obstruction to be overcome. For every Catlin who fretted about the future of the buffalo, dozens more yearned to kill as many of these creatures as possible. "The wonders of inanimate nature leave [Americans] cold," observed Alexis de Tocqueville, a Frenchman who toured the United States in the 1830s. "They do not see the admirable forests that surround them until the trees fall to their axes."[24]

As a group, then, Americans were not ready to hear, let alone to heed, the concerns of Catlin, Marsh, and other early advocates of nature and the environment. Though these thinkers had planted the seeds of the environmental movement, several more decades would pass before the seeds would begin to bear fruit.

Chapter Two

The Conservation Movement

The second half of the 1800s brought many changes to the United States. Two were particularly important to the environmental movement: a sharp increase in population and a steady improvement in technology. With more people and better machinery, the negative effects of human activity on nature were difficult to ignore. It became increasingly evident, for example, that George Perkins Marsh was right when he claimed that humans could seriously harm the natural world. Similarly, Henry David Thoreau's notion that nature had a right to exist no longer seemed so far fetched. During the 1880s and 1890s naturalists, artists, and political leaders began to accept—and to implement—the ideas of early environmentalists like Marsh and Thoreau.

From a modern perspective, it is fair to say that this second wave of environmentalists had limited goals. They paid little or no attention to important envi-

ronmental problems such as air pollution. Nor did they do much to help distressed ecosystems in regions where significant environmental damage had already been done. And for the most part they had no interest in urging Americans to use fewer resources, whether by becoming less wasteful of energy or by moving away from the growing consumer culture of the time. At this point only a few Americans were prepared to tackle these difficult problems.

The environmentalists of the late 1800s *were* prepared, however, to deal with one very important issue. That was the question of conservation, or the protection of land and wildlife in its natural state. Worried that some of America's most beautiful landscapes might be lost forever to development, thinkers like naturalist John Muir and politician Theodore Roosevelt spoke out in favor of keeping these areas just as they were. In this regard they were quite successful. The conservationists set aside millions of acres of land for public use, helped prevent the extinction of several species, and—perhaps most important—established the notion that people and governments alike have the obligation to act, at least at times, in the best interests of the planet.

Forests, Farms, and Extinction

Where the environment was concerned, most Americans of the 1860s and 1870s continued to follow the lead of their parents and grandparents. Just as New Englanders had cut down extensive tracts of trees during colonial times and the early 1800s, so too did Midwesterners steadily raze their forests fifty or seventy-five years later. "When a man started to clear a piece of land he chopped down *every tree on it*," wrote Indiana author Gene Stratton Porter of her 1860s childhood, "in order that he might use the land for the growing of wheat, corn, and potatoes."[25]

As the forests disappeared, so did animals. With the passage of time and with westward expansion, more and more species were in danger of dying out altogether. In the early 1800s, for example, the passenger pigeon was perhaps the most numerous bird species in America. These birds traveled in flocks estimated to contain hundreds of millions of birds.

Settlers shoot at a flock of passenger pigeons. The species became extinct because the settlers frequently hunted them for sport and destroyed the forests where they lived.

"The air was literally filled with pigeons," wrote John James Audubon of a flock he saw in 1813. "The light of noonday was obscured as by an eclipse."[26] But as settlers moved west, they killed millions of the birds as pests, shot millions more for food or for sport, and converted the forests where the pigeons nested into farmland. By 1880 the species was on its way to extinction.

The buffalo was another example. Most Americans of the 1830s and 1840s scoffed at George Catlin's prediction that the buffalo would eventually become extinct. Though by the 1840s hardly any buffalo continued to live east of the Mississippi, the Great Plains had no shortage of them. As late as 1871, for instance, a group of soldiers encountered an unusually large group of buffalo on the plains of Kansas. "For six days," reported an officer, "we continued our way through this enormous herd. . . . [It was] impossible to approximate the millions."[27]

In reality, though, the buffalo's numbers were already dwindling. Newcomers to the West were eager to eradicate the buffalo and turn the Great Plains into wheat farms or grazing land for cattle. Hunters flocked to the region, often shooting at the animals from the safety of train windows. Thanks to improved weaponry and what one writer of the time described as the buffalo's "phenomenal stupidity,"[28] a hunter could kill dozens of buffalo in a single day. One man was said to have killed over a thousand in a single six-week period. Occasionally the hunters ate their kill. More often, they shot the buffalo for sport and left the carcasses to rot. By 1890 only a few hundred buffalo remained in the wild.

Changes

Most Americans of the 1860s and 1870s shed no tears over the slaughter of the buffalo, the extinction of the passenger pigeon, and the destruction of forests. Like earlier generations, most Americans of this period still viewed nature as a resource to be used—or to be tossed aside if it had no particular value. If the presence of the buffalo on the Great Plains thwarted Americans' dreams of building cattle ranches in the West, then the buffalo had to be removed—it was as simple as that. If farmers in Indiana wanted to cultivate more land, they had the right to chop down all the trees they wanted. The ecological consequences of these activities bothered them not at all.

But not every American of this period held that view. Where men like Marsh and Catlin had once been members of a tiny minority, their ideas were now beginning to spread. As the 1870s moved into the 1880s and 1890s, more and more people were finding America's scenery, wildlife, and landforms valuable in themselves. Some observers focused on the natural beauty of the land. "America is fast being recognized as holding within her grasp grander and more beautiful things than any other land under the sun,"[29] boasted one commentator in 1881. Others criticized human activities that involved destruction for its own sake. A writer of the 1880s, for example, complained that the mass killing of buffalo was "unsportsmanlike, unfair, ignoble,

Tourists admire the natural beauty of the Great Geyser Basin at Yellowstone Park in the 1880s.

and utterly reprehensible"[30]—a charge that few would have leveled against the hunters of earlier eras.

This shift in American attitudes toward the natural world came about for several reasons. Most obviously, the United States was far from the same country in 1880 than it had been eight or even four decades earlier. Population had risen dramatically: It had tripled from 1800 to 1840, and nearly tripled again in the next forty years. New machines enabled farmers to clear more land and plant more crops. Factories sprang up to churn out goods from barrels to blankets. Railroads, almost unknown in 1830s America, now stretched from the Atlantic to the Pacific. The combination of more people and better technology caused more environmental damage—and more noticeable damage as well.

Another consideration played a role as well: the magnificence of the American West. Most Americans acknowledged that the East had its share of natural beauty. Niagara Falls on the New York–Canadian border was widely admired. So was Mount Monadnock in New Hampshire, which was one of Thoreau's favorite places. Mammoth Cave in Kentucky, wrote one early visitor, was "the monarch of caves. . . . In wild, solemn, severe, unadorned majesty, it stands alone."[31] From the Florida Keys to the bluffs of Wisconsin, the East had dozens of beautiful and interesting places.

But compared to the West, the East seemed tame and uninspiring. The mountains of the West were taller and craggier, the wildlife more majestic, the landscapes more breathtaking. The West, it was clear, was a national treasure, and the glories of these lands awakened not just national pride but a protective instinct in many Americans. To some observers, the most beautiful areas of the West were works of art, worthy of the same respect as the cathedrals of Europe. Certainly, many Americans agreed, parts of the West should remain as nature had made them. As one man wrote of the Yellowstone region in Wyoming, "The intelligent American will one day point on the map to this remarkable district with the conscious pride that it has not its parallel on the face of the earth"[32]—assuming, he warned, that it survived intact.

Yosemite and Yellowstone

The conservation movement had its first real success in 1864. Not surprisingly, the success came in the West—specifically, the breathtakingly beautiful Yosemite Valley of California. In a land filled with the glories of nature, Yosemite was often agreed to be the best of the best. *"Enchanting! Awe-inspiring! Indescribable!"* raved the entry about Yosemite in an 1872 guidebook. The valley had "the grandest scenery on the American continent, if not in the world"; it "presents a scene of beauty and magnificence un-

surpassed, except *possibly* in childhood's fairy dreams."[33] Public opinion strongly favored setting this land aside as a public park, and in June 1864 Congress approved a bill to do exactly that. According to the new law, much of the valley and its surroundings now belonged to the State of California, reserved "for public use, resort and recreation . . . for all time."[34]

Delighted to have protected Yosemite from development, conservationists now tried to protect another marvel: Yellowstone, a mountainous area centered in northwestern Wyoming. Like Yosemite, Yellowstone was famous for its beauty. "As genius in mental matters stands above mediocrity," wrote a reporter in 1886, "so does the scenery on the headwaters above the Yellowstone River stand high above that of [an] ordinary mortal's view."[35] Yellowstone, however, was also home to geysers, hot springs, and unusual rock formations, many of which visitors found unpleasant or even sinister. "Horrible mud volcanoes, and pools of black, boiling mud alternate with fairy-like terraces,"[36] wrote one early visitor in wonderment, summing up the two faces of Yellowstone.

As with Yosemite the notion of setting aside Yellowstone for public use faced little opposition. Backers of this plan assured congressional leaders that the land had no practical value. Yellowstone would never be suitable for agriculture, they promised; nor did anyone think it had usable minerals. In 1872 Congress designated Yellowstone a public park, to be run by the federal government.

An illustration depicts Yosemite Valley in the 1870s. The land was reserved as a public park in 1864.

George Catlin's desire to set aside land where the buffalo could live in peace had finally been heeded—and as Catlin had predicted, establishing a park kept the species from extinction. Of the estimated three hundred buffalo still in the wild in 1891, virtually all lived within Yellowstone's boundaries.

After the founding of Yosemite and Yellowstone, however, the conservation movement stalled. For the rest of the 1870s and the entire 1880s, Congress established no further national parks—even as the debasing of nature throughout the United States continued. Still, a precedent had been set. The federal government now had a legitimate interest in the environment. Both in California and Wyoming, the United States had taken action to protect the natural world from human interference. To several influential thinkers of the late 1800s, there was no obvious reason that it could not do so again.

John Muir

One of the most important of these thinkers was naturalist and author John Muir. Born in Scotland in 1838, Muir grew up there and in Wisconsin, where his parents moved when he was eleven. As a young man Muir walked a thou-

The Progressive Era

The 1890s and early 1900s were known as the Progressive Era. The Progressive Era was an optimistic time, a period when anything seemed possible. It was a time, as historians Allan M. Nevins and Henry Steele Commager put it, "marked by revolt and reform in almost every department of American life." In the arts, in commerce, and in politics, people were discarding old ideas and trying out new ones. Many of these ideas, moreover, were designed to create a better society for everyone. During these years, political leaders tried to eliminate poverty, stop child labor, and create more honest and responsive government.

In their support of the environment, men like John Muir and Theodore Roosevelt were squarely a part of Progressive thought. They rejected the notion that businesses had the right to destroy nature as they pleased, and they looked toward a new and better future by declaring that nature should always be a consideration when people made decisions. The conservationists of the turn of the century, then, were acting in accordance with the attitudes of their time.

Allan M. Nevins and Henry Steele Commager, *A Pocket History of the United States.* New York: Pocket, 1976, p. 336.

An illustration represents Yosemite Valley, whose natural beauty was celebrated by many environmentalists, including John Muir.

sand miles across the southern United States. Thereafter he spent most of his time traveling and enjoying the wonders of nature. For Muir a day spent hiking in the cold, pouring rain was preferable to a day inside. His writings are filled with musings about the natural world and its beauty. "The clearest way into the Universe," he once wrote, "is through a forest wilderness."[37]

Moreover, Muir had an uncompromising view of nature's role in the world. More than anyone before him, he rejected the notion that nature existed for the benefit of people. To Muir humanity was simply a part of creation, no more important than any other being. "The universe would be incomplete without man," he wrote; "but it would also be incomplete without the smallest transmicroscopic creature that dwells beyond our . . . eyes and knowledge."[38] This conviction underlies most of Muir's thinking, and it spurred him to work on behalf of the planet.

Muir loved almost any part of the natural world, but most of all he loved the mountains of California. From 1868 on he spent much of his time in and around Yosemite, writing extensively about the region and introducing thousands of Americans to the park's wonders. But while Muir celebrated the natural world of Yosemite, he worried that its beauty could not last. The park encompassed only part of the Yosemite Valley, and human use in other areas of the valley threatened its health. Farmers allowed their animals to graze the forest floors until they were nearly bare. Loggers felled trees on nearby mountains. New towns and roads pushed up against the park's borders. "The glory is departing,"[39] Muir mourned at one point.

Rather than accept the changes, Muir resolved to fight them. Between 1880 and 1890 he published any number of articles advocating for the California wilderness. His solution was simple: an expanded park like Yellowstone, managed and owned by the federal government. He pointed out that the existing park protected only one piece of a large wilderness, though in fact all the parts of the wilderness were interconnected. "The branching [canyons] and valleys of . . . the streams that pour into the Yosemite," he noted, "are as closely related to it as are the fingers to the palm of the hand." Only by enlarging the protected area, Muir argued, could the valley be kept in pristine condition. Expanding its boundaries, Muir wrote, would make the park "an harmonious unit rather than a fragment."[40]

Muir's advocacy paid off. In 1890 Congress transferred ownership of Yosemite Park to the national government and dramatically expanded its borders. But Muir did not stop there. In 1891 he helped convince congressional leaders to protect several more wilderness regions covering millions of acres. The following year he cofounded the Sierra Club, a conservation group dedicated to preserving the California mountains—and by extension, wilderness everywhere. Later he wrote several books about the mountains and the need for parkland. No one of his time worked harder—or more successfully— than Muir on behalf of the environment.

The Role of Government

Muir's achievements were hard won, for his opponents were powerful. Many large companies argued against setting aside land for national parks and forests. They complained that preserving the land would cost them money and would reduce the American standard of living. Lumber companies demanded the right to cut down trees wherever they chose. Oil companies foresaw shortages and higher prices if they could not drill where they thought best. Muir believed that conservation was morally and ethically correct— he liked to refer to the conservationist struggle as "the universal battle between right and wrong"[41]—but he understood these companies' desire for profits, and he knew he was up against a well-funded and well-organized opposition.

This opposition was why Muir made sure to bring his struggle to political leaders. Government involvement, he believed, was the key to meaningful change. "Any fool can destroy trees,"[42] he wrote at one point, urging the government to intervene on behalf of the wilderness. "God has cared for [America's] trees, saved them from drought, disease, avalanches, and a thousand straining, leveling tempests and floods; but he cannot save them from fools—only Uncle Sam can do that."[43] Without sympathetic listeners in government, Muir knew he would have no success achieving his goals.

Luckily for Muir, he did have some supporters with political power. Chief among these was Theodore Roosevelt, who became president when William McKinley was shot to death in 1901. Born

John Burroughs on Nature

John Burroughs was a naturalist best known for his descriptions of the ecology of New York State's Catskill Mountains and Hudson River Valley. He is also remembered today for a brief summary of why nature is important, quoted below, which originally appeared in his 1908 book Leaf and Tendril:

If I were to name the three most precious resources of life, I should say books, friends, and nature; and the greatest of these, at least the most constant and always at hand, is nature. Nature we have always with us, an inexhaustible storehouse of that which moves the heart, appeals to the mind, and fires the imagination—health to the body, a stimulus to the intellect, and joy to the soul. To the scientist, nature is a storehouse of facts, laws, processes; to the artist she is a storehouse of pictures; to the poet she is a storehouse of images, fancies, a source of inspiration . . . ; to all, she may be a source of knowledge and joy.

Quoted in Farida A. Wiley, ed., *John Burroughs' America*. New York: Devin-Adair, 1951, p. 16.

A photograph shows naturalists John Burroughs and John Muir seated on large rocks.

A hand-colored engraving illustrates naturalist John Muir. Muir strongly believed in the morality of environmental conservation.

in New York in 1858, Roosevelt was an eager outdoorsman. As a young man, he had lived on a ranch in the Dakota Territory and visited many of the great attractions of the West. Even after entering politics Roosevelt enjoyed the outdoors whenever he could. Indeed, when Roosevelt learned that McKinley had been shot, he was climbing Mount Marcy in New York's Adirondack wilderness—the highest peak in the state.

Wilderness and Wildlife

Roosevelt's love for America's wilderness made him an ally of those who wanted to protect the natural world. As governor of New York, he had criticized businesses that damaged the environment in search of higher profits. "Unrestrained greed means the ruin of the great woods and the drying up of the source of the rivers,"[44] he charged. Moreover, Roosevelt not only believed in protecting the natural world, he also believed that conservation was a proper role for government. "I would like to see all harmless wild things . . . protected in every way," he wrote in 1899. "I do not understand how any man or woman who really loves nature can fail to try to exert all influence in support of such [goals]."[45]

Upon becoming president, Roosevelt continued his support for nature and the wilderness. In 1903, for example, he visited the Grand Canyon for the first time. "Leave it as it is," he told the people of Arizona in a speech. "You can not improve on it. . . . Keep it for your children, your children's children, and for all who come after you."[46] During Roosevelt's administration he signed legislation to make the Grand Canyon a national monument, protecting it in the way he had advocated. In addition, he set aside three large areas in the West as national parks—Crater Lake in Oregon, Wind Cave in South Dakota, and Mesa Verde

Muir and Roosevelt in Yosemite

In 1903, at Theodore Roosevelt's request, Roosevelt and John Muir spent three days together camping in Yosemite and visiting the sequoias, among the biggest and oldest trees on Earth. Roosevelt's autobiography described the experience as follows:

The first night was clear, and we lay down in the darkening aisles of the great Sequoia grove. The majestic trunks, beautiful in color and in symmetry, rose round us like the pillars of a mightier cathedral than ever was conceived even by the fervor [enthusiasm] of the Middle Ages. Hermit thrushes sang beautifully in the evening, and again, with a burst of wonderful music, at dawn.

I was interested and a little surprised to find that . . . John Muir cared little for birds or bird songs, and knew little about them. The hermit thrushes meant nothing to him, the trees and the flowers and the cliffs everything. . . . The second night we camped in a snowstorm, on the edge of the [canyon] walls, under the spreading limbs of a grove of mighty silver fir; and next day we went down into the wonderland of the valley itself. I shall always be glad that I was in the Yosemite with John Muir.

Theodore Roosevelt, "In Yosemite with John Muir," Sierra Club. www.sierraclub.org/ john_muir_exhibit/frameindex.html? http://www.sierraclub.org/john_Muir_ex hibit/life/in_yosemite _by_roosevelt.html.

Theodore Roosevelt and John Muir stand on Glacier Point above Yosemite Valley. The two men camped together in Yosemite for three days.

in Colorado. Finally, Roosevelt ordered the protection of thousands of acres of land as part of the national forest system. On one memorable day in 1907, he created twenty-one new forest reserves in the northwestern states alone and enlarged the borders of eleven more.

A snowy egret is pictured at the Everglades National Park in Florida. In the 1900s, Theodore Roosevelt asked the government for protection of the egret species and other wildlife.

Roosevelt also acted on behalf of wildlife. During the early 1900s women often wore fancy hats that incorporated the feathers of various bird species. To meet the demand for feathers, hunters shot thousands upon thousands of birds, focusing especially on those with colorful or striking feathers. The result was predictable: The birds with the most prized plumage began to die out. The feather trade was so lucrative that hunters regularly disobeyed the few laws against shooting birds.

Then in 1905 hunters in Florida killed several egrets—one of the most valuable of all birds at the time and one that in Florida, at least, had legal protection. When a game warden tried to arrest them, the hunters shot and killed him as well. Roosevelt was one of many who was outraged by the hunters' actions. He urged legislators to increase penalties against hunters who broke the law, discourage the hat industry from using feathers, and provide greater protections for the birds. He led by example, too, designating an island off the coast of Florida as a sanctuary where birds could not be shot. "Is there any law that will prevent me from declaring Pelican Island a Federal Bird Reservation?" Roosevelt is said to have asked his staff. "Very well," he continued when the answer was no, "then I so declare it."[47]

The End of an Era
Politically speaking, Roosevelt and Muir did not always see eye to eye. Muir wanted to keep protected lands as unspoiled as possible, which meant permitting mainly low-impact human activities

A photograph depicts the Hetch Hetchy Reservoir. Amidst much controversy, the Hetch Hetchy Valley was flooded in the 1920s to provide a water supply for the growing city of San Francisco.

such as hiking and small-scale hunting and fishing. Roosevelt, in contrast, was eager to allow more intensive hunting and fishing, and he also advocated some commercial use of national parks and forests. He did not mind logging in protected areas, for example, as long as the logging left the bulk of a forest standing and did little damage to the rest of the ecosystem. "Preserve the forests," he urged his Grand Canyon audience. "Preserve them for the ranchman and the stockman . . . for the people of the region round about. Preserve them for that use, but use them so they will not be squandered, that they will not be wasted."[48]

The differences between the two men became most glaring in what proved to be Muir's final battle. Government leaders in California wanted a reliable water supply for the growing city of San Francisco. In 1906 they proposed building a dam that would create a reservoir. The dam, however, would flood the Hetch Hetchy Valley near Yosemite and destroy it. Muir, who believed that Hetch Hetchy was one of the most beautiful places on Earth, found this plan intolerable. The

Commercialism and the Parks

M any who supported a system of national parks did so for commercial reasons. True, the mountains of the West seemed to have no particular economic worth, and those who advocated keeping places such as Yellowstone as they were emphasized that the soil was no good for farming and that the rocks seemed to contain no minerals of any value. Still, those who lived near prospective national parkland believed they could make money by attracting tourists to these wilderness areas.

The United States of the late 1800s was much wealthier than it had been two or three generations earlier. Given increasingly good transportation and more disposable income, tourism had become common. New settlers to the West hoped to build hotels, railroads, and stores to meet the needs of the travelers who would come visit the great unspoiled sections of America. As one California booster pointed out, preserving Yosemite would provide "a source of wealth to the whole community." Indeed, the national parks soon became a popular destination for tourists, enabling thousands of local people to earn a more comfortable living.

Quoted in John F. Sears, *Sacred Places*. New York: Oxford University Press, 1989, p. 130.

officials who backed this plan, he charged, "seem to have a perfect contempt for Nature."[49] But Roosevelt did not share Muir's anger. He wanted to encourage San Francisco's growth, which he thought would help the United States economically, and saw no ecologically friendly way to provide the city with water. In the end Muir lost the battle, and Hetch Hetchy disappeared under the waters.

Roosevelt left the presidency in 1909 and died ten years later. Muir died in California in 1914, the same year, as it happened, that the passenger pigeon became extinct. Together, the two men had done as much as anyone to protect America's wilderness. Their methods were different, of course, and their characters were, too. Muir was more of a philosopher and a Thoreau-style loner, Roosevelt a pragmatist who loved the world of politics. But the men had much in common as well. Both were genuine in their love of nature. Both worked to ensure that mountains and forests of their time would survive to delight future generations. And both were optimistic that their views would ultimately prevail. As Muir put it late in life, speaking of his opponents, "They will see what I meant in time. There must be places for human beings to satisfy their souls. Food and drink is not all."[50] Roosevelt, no doubt, would have agreed.

Chapter Three

Science and the Environment

T he conservation movement of the late 1800s and early 1900s valued open lands in large part for aesthetic reasons—that is, because they were scenic and serene. John Muir and Theodore Roosevelt not only emphasized the stunning beauty of much of the American West, each also described nature in spiritual terms that verged on the mystic. "All the world seems a church and the mountains altars,"[51] wrote Muir at one point. Even the more pragmatic Roosevelt agreed; he once described the experience of camping at Yosemite as being "like lying in a great solemn cathedral, far vaster and more beautiful than any built by the hand of man."[52]

To be sure, the conservation movement had a scientific aspect as well. Following the lead of earlier thinkers like George Perkins Marsh, some Americans of the time relied on biological arguments to make the case for conserving lands and wildlife. They understood that the removal of the Midwestern forests, for example, helped lead to the extinction of the passenger pigeon; they saw that excessive fishing could harm the populations of animals that fed upon the fish. Like Marsh, these thinkers pointed out that people affected the world in unexpected ways. Still, the conservation movement of Muir's and Roosevelt's time was not primarily based on science. In arguing for the natural world, conservationists of the period appealed more to the senses and the spirit than to scientific studies and experimental data.

That would change, however. During the 1950s and 1960s, the environmental movement became increasingly based on science. Activists researched the impact of air pollution and studied how chemicals affected birds, rodents, and people. They studied the needs of wild animals and how national policy met—or failed to meet—those needs. They investigated the consequences of drilling for oil, building a power plant, or tearing up a meadow to construct a housing development. What they learned was important, unexpected, and sometimes alarming. The years from 1950 through the late 1960s, then, were notable for bringing science into the debate over the environment.

Lean Years

The years after 1909, when Theodore Roosevelt left office, were not good ones for the environmental movement. Other than expanding the list of national parks and forests to include scenic regions like Acadia in Maine, Bryce Canyon in Utah, and Michigan's Isle Royale, the attentions of Americans and their leaders largely turned away from environmental concerns. To some degree, they believed their work was done. Yellowstone's geysers and hot springs were now protected, as were Yosemite's cliffs and valleys. The buffalo had been saved, even if its numbers remained low, and laws protected bird species that had once been hunted for their feathers. True, the passenger pigeon was gone for good, along with several other species; but many Americans viewed these losses, if they thought of them at all, as mistakes that could never occur again.

More immediate needs played a role, too. In 1914 World War I broke out, and while the United States did not join the fighting until 1917, the nation was consumed for several years with questions

The 1920s

The 1920s were a prosperous time in the United States. Incomes were rising, though mainly for the richest Americans; industries were growing rapidly. The 1920s included some cultural innovation—jazz music, for example, became widely popular for the first time—but unlike the Progressive Era of a generation before, it was not a period of change and experimentation where politics and economics were concerned.

The 1920s, indeed, were known for an extremely practical outlook on the world. Generally speaking, Americans of the 1920s opposed reform, viewed new ideas with suspicion, and rejected the idealism of earlier times. What was good for business, many believed, was good for the country. As Allan M. Nevins and Henry Steele Commager write, "Never before had the government of the United States been more unabashedly the instrument of privileged groups." This was not a climate in which environmentalism could easily flourish—and not surprisingly, it did not.

Allan M. Nevins and Henry Steele Commager, *A Pocket History of the United States.* New York: Pocket, 1976, p. 408.

The Appalachian Trail footpath provides scenic views of surrounding nature for Americans.

of war and international politics. The Great Depression of the 1930s threw millions of people out of work, and the early 1940s were the years of American involvement in World War II. Next to these crises, environmental issues faded into the background. During these difficult times, Americans' energies were focused on winning wars and restoring prosperity—not on saving endangered species and ending water pollution.

Even during the leanest times, though, environmentalists still spoke up for their cause and sought to help the natural world. The Appalachian Trail, a footpath stretching from Georgia to Maine, was completed in 1937, providing recreation and scenic views to millions of Americans. In the early 1930s, moreover, President Franklin Roosevelt established several organizations devoted to environmental issues such as soil erosion. And some Americans questioned the environmental impact of nuclear weapons tests in the late 1940s and early 1950s. Still, the general attitude toward the environment between 1910 and the 1950s was one of neglect.

A New Era

The 1950s and early 1960s, however, were a new and different time. The country was at peace and growing prosperous. Standards of living were rising rapidly; education levels were increasing. Moreover, the United States was becoming a technological powerhouse. Work crews dynamited hillsides to make room for roads and houses. American factories manufactured steel, cars, chemicals, plastics, and thousands of other goods, often working overtime to keep up with the demand. Americans had come a long way from the days of colonization, when they were at the mercy of the natural world around them. Now, it seemed, they were in control.

The new technologies *were* exciting. According to many thinkers, chemicals, rocket fuel, and mass production promised a bright future for everyone. Practically all social and scientific problems, it seemed, could be solved. Scientists and politicians alike assumed that technological progress would soon make it easy to do things long believed impossible, such as conquering cancer or traveling to the outer reaches of the solar system. "We're 20 years away from a colony on Mars,"[53] one scientist stated confidently (if erroneously) in 1960.

At the same time, though, the increasing reliance on technology made some Americans uneasy. They wondered if these technologies carried hidden costs: health risks to humans, potential problems for the environment. Everyone agreed, for example, that factory smoke was an annoyance, but activists began to wonder if it lowered life expectancies for people who breathed too much of it. What, exactly, was in all those chemicals that found their way into foods and medicines? Could these ingredients harm people? What about the effect on birds and mammals, and what about the impact on forests, fields, and rivers? As the 1940s and 1950s wore on, questions like these became more and more common.

Tragedy in Donora

Several incidents helped spark these questions. One early example was an event that took place in the manufacturing community of Donora, Pennsylvania. Located along a river near Pittsburgh, Donora was home to several

A smoky factory in Donora, Pennsylvania, is pictured. In 1948 pollution and smog from Donora's factories covered the city and resulted in the deaths of twenty people.

factories that employed most of the town's workers. When the factories were running, thick, heavy smoke filled the air around the town. The smoke was smelly and unpleasant, but the people of Donora rarely complained. To them, dirty air was a sign of good economic times. Plumes of smoke indicated that the factories had orders to fill and were willing and able to hire laborers. As workers in factory towns across America liked to say, the smell of smoke was "the smell of money."[54]

Though Donora had no more factories than many other towns, the smoke in Donora was worse than almost anywhere else. The reason was geography. Donora was located in a narrow valley, and cliffs on each side of the river often blocked winds from dispersing the pollution. During the fall, especially, smoke sometimes barely moved after pouring out of the factory smokestacks. The people of Donora knew to expect occasional autumn days when the smoke was particularly bad. Those who had breathing problems made sure to stay indoors on those days. Before long, though, the weather typically would change and the smoke would be gone.

No one in Donora, though, was prepared for what happened in the fall of 1948. On October 26, the town began to fill with smog—a thick combination of fog and factory smoke. The smog soon covered everything. "There never was such a fog," reported firefighter Russell Davis. "You couldn't see your hand in front of your face, day or night." All over Donora, even people who were gener-

ally healthy began coughing, vomiting, and gasping for breath. It seemed to many as if the smog were driving oxygen out of the air and poisoning their systems. "I don't know how I kept breathing," Davis recalled, noting that the smoke penetrated the fire station and other public buildings. "I don't know how anybody did."[55]

The smog was heavier and longer lasting than ever before in Donora's history. Over the next six days, thousands sought medical treatment. Nearly half the population of the town became sick, and twenty people died. Factory owners, unwilling to accept blame for the disaster, insisted that they had not released poisonous chemicals into Donora's air. An official investigation agreed that "no single substance was responsible for the . . . episode,"[56] but nonetheless concluded that the factories were to blame. The smoke plumes, the report read, contained any number of potentially dangerous substances. Most likely, some of these substances had come together in the smog to create a new and toxic material.

The Donora tragedy made people across the country think twice about the factories in their own regions—and wonder what toxic chemicals the smoke from these mills might contain. Immediately after the disaster, one Pennsylvania newspaper called for the closing of Donora's factories if the mills were truly at fault. "The economic effects of such action . . . may be difficult at first," the writer conceded, recognizing that people in the region relied on the factories for work, "but Donora will be a better town in every way if this blight is lifted."[57] Others went further, arguing that governments needed to protect their citizens. "The air is public property," editorialized an Iowa newspaper in the wake of the tragedy, "and no private individual or industry has the right to pollute it to the extent that public health is endangered."[58]

Over the next few years, concern about air pollution intensified. Scientists ran tests on the smoke plumes that spread out from American factories and studied the effects of the smoke on nearby areas. Their results were not comforting. In town after town the studies showed that air pollution had strongly negative effects. By the late 1950s, for instance, scientists recognized that people who lived in heavily polluted areas were more likely to get lung cancer. In some states chemical discharges cracked and discolored house paint; studies revealed that moisture in the air had converted the fumes into acid. Sulfur dioxide, soot, zinc, carbon monoxide—all were present in factory smoke, and all were toxic. Science had made it clear that air pollution was much more harmful than most people had suspected.

Parks, Power Plants, and Sprawl

The growing field of environmental science did not focus exclusively on air pollution; in the years after World War II, environmentalists used science in other ways as well. During this period, for example, conservationists frequently urged Congress to expand the boundaries of

several national parks. One reason they gave was that expansion would help animals such as the wolf and the grizzly bear. Research had shown that wolves, for example, roamed a far larger territory than earlier activists had believed. This enormous range meant that these animals often strayed beyond the boundaries of national parkland, where they were at risk of being shot. "The parks are certainly too small for such a far-ranging species as the wolf,"[59] summed up one advocate—an argument that would have been difficult to make before biologists began studying the wolf in detail.

Another example had to do with a controversy over Storm King Mountain along the Hudson River. In the early 1960s a New York City utility company announced plans to build a power plant at the base of the mountain. The project involved digging a tunnel under Storm King and removing a part of the mountainside. Local residents, however, objected. Part of their argument was aesthetic. Storm King was an important landmark, the opponents said, which anchored an exceptionally beautiful part of the Hudson River. "It rises like a brown bear out of the water," argued one advocate, using language that would have pleased Thoreau, "a dome of living granite, swelling with animal power."[60] For these people the matter seemed simple: Storm King's spiritual and artistic value outweighed its value as a site for a power plant.

However, Storm King's defenders did not focus exclusively on nature and beauty. They also brought up scientific

Controversy surrounded Storm King Mountain in the early 1960s when a utility company wanted to build a power plant at the mountain's base.

arguments. At one point, for example, they hired biologists to predict how the river's fish might be affected by a new power plant. The biologists reported that fish would likely become entangled in water intake pipes or killed by whirling generators. Opponents of the project also noted that the plant would discharge heat into the atmosphere and into the Hudson as well, and questioned the effect of this heat on the environment. Both strategies were successful; the utility ultimately lost the battle, and Storm King remained intact.

A third example had to do with a new phenomenon in post–World War II America: urban sprawl. Throughout most of American history, cities were typically compact, with suburban areas lying close to the city's boundaries. In the 1950s, though, new suburbs began to spring up at some distance from the cities. Urban areas became larger and less densely populated. While many of America's new suburbanites liked the increased open space and did not object to long daily commutes, the sprawling urban areas created environmental issues. In particular, the landscape changed as bulldozers knocked down hills, tore up fields, and filled in swamps to make room for houses, schools, and roads.

During the late 1950s some observers began to view urban sprawl with alarm.

As with Storm King and the national parks, critics of this practice used scientific arguments to make their case. Alongside pleas to spare the nation's natural beauty, environmentalists attacked sprawl because it caused specific problems for the Earth. That was especially true for wetlands, such as swamps and other marshy areas. Animals such as frogs and muskrats needed wetlands to stay alive, environmentalists noted; filling in marshes and swamps could destroy these animal populations. Moreover, excess water collected in wetlands during times of heavy rains. Without wetlands, water would have no safe place to drain, making housing developments much more prone to floods. "Scientists say, for nature's sake—and for man's sake—don't blacktop it all,"[61] argued one environmentalist.

Insect Control

Perhaps the most important scientific controversy of the time, though, had to do with insects. Insects have caused great harm to human beings throughout history. Many species bite, sting, and spread disease. Others destroy crops.

Until quite recently, people could do little to control insects. In the late 1800s, though, the chemical industry began developing substances that were toxic to many insect species. When sprayed on a farm field, these substances killed pests that attacked and ate the crops. When sprayed in towns and cities, they killed insects that bit, stung, and spread disease. During the early 1900s these poisons, known as pesticides or insecticides, became increasingly powerful and pop-

ular. By World War II several highly effective pesticides were available for household use. "Make INSECT-O-BLITZ profits ring the cash register for you—now!"[62] read an ad for one of these products, urging retailers to stock pesticides for sale to ordinary consumers.

Many Americans thoroughly approved of these new chemicals. By the 1950s it was clear that pesticides worked. Insect populations were down sharply. Farmers relaxed, secure in the belief that pests not devour their crops. Mosquito-borne diseases were on the decrease, and outdoor recreation was becoming more enjoyable. "This was the first summer when we did not actually need screen doors,"[63] marveled a Kansas resident in 1946, soon after his community sprayed pesticides for the first time. Experts in the chemical industry boasted of having eliminated certain pests from parts of the United States altogether and looked forward to the extermination of others. Given enough time and enough insecticide, they believed, even the common housefly could be wiped out.

But not everyone was so enthusiastic. Some Americans worried that chemicals that killed insects might also be dangerous to other living things. What poisoned bugs could very well poison crops, they argued, or birds or deer or even people. This concern was not just theoretical: As early as the 1940s a few people claimed that insecticides were harming their health. "Our home is in a smother of poisons from surrounding farms from early spring until late autumn," complained one woman in 1949. "Our continued illness . . .

A plant protection expert sprays potato crops with chemicals. Many environmentalists worried that pesticides could damage other wildlife, even though the chemicals killed the insects that attacked crops.

E.B. White on the Environment

E.B. White, the author of the children's classic Charlotte's Web, *was an early advocate for the Earth, as the following excerpt demonstrates. White wrote these words in 1956, shortly after President Dwight Eisenhower gave a speech in which he praised the "smoky fury" of American factories and called the smoke a sign of prosperity.*

I [believe] that no rat poison is the correct amount to spread in the kitchen where children and puppies can get at it. I believe that no chemical waste is the correct amount to discharge into the fresh rivers of the world, and I believe that if there is a way to trap the fumes from factory chimneys, it should be against the law to set these deadly fumes adrift where they can mingle with fog and, given the right conditions, suddenly turn an area into another Donora, Pa. . . . I can see the smoky fury of our factories drifting right into this room this very minute; the fury sits in my throat like a bundle of needles, it explores my nose, chokes off my breath, and makes my eyes burn. The room smells like a slaughterhouse. And the phenomenon gets [only] a brief mention in the morning press.

Quoted in Bill McKibben, ed., *American Earth: Environmental Writing Since Thoreau.* New York: Library of America, 2008, p. 331.

Children's author E.B. White advocated environmentalism.

has occurred after being exposed to these poison mists and sprays."[64] The insecticide industry dismissed such claims, arguing that pesticides did not have negative effects if used properly. Still, questions persisted.

Rachel Carson and *Silent Spring*

The most important of these questioners was a scientist and author named Rachel Carson. Born in 1907, Carson became known in the 1950s for several books about the oceans and marine life. A trained biologist and a skilled writer, she combined a scientist's understanding of the processes of nature with a John Muir–like love for the natural world, and her books proved extremely popular. Indeed, her book *The Sea Around Us* appeared on the *New York Times* best-seller list for nearly two years.

Soon after World War II, spurred by concerns about America's rising technologies, Carson began studying the effects of insecticides. Her particular interest was a chemical known as DDT, widely used by American farmers to keep pests from eating their crops. Other scientists had investigated aspects of DDT use and its effect on the environment, but no one had yet gone through the studies one by one and connected their conclusions. In the late 1950s and early 1960s, Carson reviewed the data and came to an unsettling conclusion: The impact of DDT was not by any means limited to insects.

In 1962 Carson revealed her findings in her best-known work, *Silent Spring*.

In her book Silent Spring, *author and biologist Rachel Carson revealed the damaging properties the chemical DDT had on the environment.*

Citing study after study, Carson made it clear that DDT was damaging the environment—possibly beyond repair. When fish, mammals, or birds ate insects or plants that had been sprayed by DDT, she noted, the chemical remained in their systems and settled into their organs and body tissues. The more they ate, the more the chemicals built up. Under some circumstances, the level of DDT in these animals' systems could reach astonishing levels. A late-1950s study in California, for example, investigated the effects on birds after a lake was sprayed with a weak concentration of DDT. The researchers were shocked to discover that the DDT in the birds' bodies was eighty thousand times stronger than the DDT in the lake.

As the poison built up, moreover, it became deadly. Carson carefully laid out the evidence that supported this conclusion, especially where birds were concerned. She pointed to dozens of communities where the bird population dropped sharply after DDT came into widespread use. She noted studies showing that birds often had trouble reproducing when farmers applied DDT to nearby fields. And she wrote about the particular threats to well-known birds like the bald eagle and the songbirds that most Americans took for granted. Indeed, Carson began her book by describing a "silent spring"—a future world in which no birds sang, because almost all had been wiped out by indiscriminate use of DDT. "It was a spring without voices," she wrote; "only silence lay over the fields and woods and marsh."[65]

Silent Spring mainly described the effects of DDT on wildlife, but Carson also questioned what impact insecticides might have on people. Some studies of the time suggested that DDT might cause cancer. Carson cited stories of agricultural workers who had become seriously ill after handling materials that had been sprayed with insecticide. "Does Indiana still raise any boys who roam through woods and fields?" she asked, noting reports that Indiana farmers had sprayed an entire rural area to eliminate pests. "If so, who guard[s] the poisoned area to keep out any who might wander in, in misguided search for unspoiled nature?"[66] For Carson and for many of her readers, the lesson was clear. It was not wise to accept the manufacturers' word that DDT and other insecticides were perfectly safe.

New Research

Chemical company officials bitterly resisted Carson's conclusions. They charged that she had misread data; they accused her of bias against corporations. They also warned that abandoning insecticides—which they believed was Carson's ultimate goal—would mean returning to "a dark age of plague and epidemic."[67] *Silent Spring*, they concluded, was less a work of science than a work of fiction. Most Americans, however, disagreed. They took *Silent Spring* seriously—especially as further scientific research emerged to support Carson's conclusions. One study, for example, determined that the peregrine falcon had virtually disappeared throughout the eastern United States, probably because of increasing pesticide use. And another study found traces of DDT in Antarctic wildlife, even though insecticides had never been used anywhere near Antarctica. "These findings," editorialized an Indiana newspaper in 1965, "emphasize once again the importance of trying to

"I Was Part of the Aurora"

Despite the scientific bent of many environmentalists in the 1950s and 1960s, some activists continued to echo thinkers such as John Muir and Henry David Thoreau. Like these men, they spoke of the beauty of the natural world and the spiritual side of being out in nature, and they championed nature's right to exist. A few, in fact, were uncomfortable with the notion that nature was fundamentally about science. In a 1956 article, for example, environmental activist Sigurd Olson described the experience of watching the aurora borealis, a natural display of lights in the night sky that occasionally can be seen in northern latitudes. "I was part of the aurora," he wrote, "part of its light and the great curtain that trembled above me." Olson knew that science had explained what the aurora was and why it appeared, but he preferred not to focus on scientific thought. "What did the scientists know about what I had done?" he demanded. "How could they explain what had happened to me and the strange sensations I had known?"

Quoted in Bill McKibben, ed., *American Earth: Environmental Writing Since Thoreau*. New York: Library of America, 2008, p. 325.

The aurora borealis shines over Manitoba, Canada. Environmental phenomena like this natural display of light caused some activists to see the spirituality in nature.

foresee possible consequences when new chemicals are put into our natural environment."[68]

The work of scientific researchers like Rachel Carson changed the way Americans thought about environmental issues—and changed the terms of the debate about the natural world. As the 1960s wore on, study after study revealed the hazards of air pollution, urban sprawl, pesticide use, and more. While some farmers, industry leaders, and others dismissed these studies and cast doubt on their conclusions, it was becoming increasingly obvious to many Americans that the natural world was in danger. "A grim specter has crept up on us almost unnoticed," wrote Carson, warning that her "silent spring" scenario "may easily become a stark reality we all shall know."[69]

Worse yet, the blame seemed to lie squarely with human action. For generations Americans had operated on the notion that the world existed primarily for human use. The scientific research of the 1950s and 1960s made it evident that this attitude was no longer appropriate. The new technologies of the twentieth century had the power to disrupt the balance of nature as never before, and the possible consequences were alarming—for wildlife and for humanity alike. After the discovery that a chemical used in laundry detergents had contaminated the water supplies of many towns, one environmentalist summed up the concerns of a growing number of Americans. "The side effects in this case interfered with our well-being and aesthetic sensibilities," he wrote. "Next time they may threaten our very survival."[70]

Chapter Four

An Environmental Revolution

By the late 1960s few serious researchers doubted that the world was under heavy attack from pesticides, pollution, and dwindling open space, among other environmental issues. Indeed, even for ordinary citizens evidence of damage to the natural world was easy to find. Sludge, chemicals, and oils were so common in waterways that Cleveland's Cuyahoga River caught fire on several occasions. Strip mining, a process in which companies pulled layers of soil off hilltops to expose the minerals beneath, was turning extensive stretches of Appalachia into wastelands. Clouds of smog still hung over Los Angeles, Pittsburgh, and dozens of other communities. And everywhere, it seemed, grasslands, hills, and lakes were being replaced by shopping centers, schools, and houses. As folk singer Joni Mitchell lamented in one of her songs, people were paving over paradise to build parking lots.

The time was ripe for an "environmental revolution,"[71] as one activist described what took place between the mid-1960s and the mid-1970s. The success of the environmental movement during this time was nothing short of astonishing. Through education, persistence, and most of all, new laws, environmental activists achieved what earlier advocates like John Muir and George Perkins Marsh had only dreamed of: a society in which environmental protection was a priority. Much of the success had to do with new laws. "Never, before or since," writes naturalist and author Scott Weidensaul, "had a nation so quickly and so fundamentally rewritten its laws to give the natural world a measure of protection."[72] But perhaps just as important, the work of the environmentalists led to remarkable changes in the way people thought about the world around them. The environmental movement of the late 1960s and early 1970s was not just about changing behaviors—it was about changing attitudes as well.

Education

The environmentalists of the late 1960s used a number of tactics to spread their message. Among the most important of these was education. For the activists of the time, an important goal was to raise Americans' awareness of the environment and its problems. They hoped to make it plain that quick and extensive action was necessary to preserve what still remained healthy in the natural world—and to repair the damage that had already been done.

Education was hardly a new strategy for the environmental movement. John Muir had written magazine articles to focus attention on conservation, after all, and Rachel Carson's books had been big sellers. But the environmentalists of the late 1960s and early 1970s focused on education in ways that earlier thinkers had not. In particular, they sought to reach as many people as possible, not just adults who read articles in magazines or bought books on scientific topics. The environmentalists of the late 1960s and early 1970s not only made education a centerpiece of their strategy, they expanded their audience as well. On both counts they were enormously successful.

The Environment and the 1960s

The late 1960s were a time of protest in America. Many Americans were very unhappy with the direction the country was taking. Much of this discontent had to do with the continued involvement of American troops in the Vietnam War, an armed conflict in southeastern Asia that the United States had joined but seemed to be losing. Plenty of Americans were also angry about racism; during this time African Americans, Hispanics, and other minorities were becoming increasingly vocal in demanding their civil rights, or the rights due to them just by being American citizens. Against this backdrop environmental policy was just another source of frustration for people who already believed their government was not doing what it should.

That frustration was especially apparent among college students and other youth. Younger protesters were in a particularly uncompromising mood. They rejected not only the government policies of the time, but the music, clothing, and hairstyles of previous generations. Anger over the way the older generation had treated the environment, then, fit right in with their general mood of discontent and fed their certainty that if they were put in charge, the country would be in much better shape.

Then...
Oh! Baby! Oh!
How my business did grow!
Now, chopping one tree
at a time
was too slow.

So I quickly invented my Super-Axe-Hacker
which whacked off four Truffula Trees at one smacker.
We were making Thneeds
four times as fast as before!
And that Lorax?...
He didn't show up any more.

A picture displays the pages from Dr. Seuss's The Lorax. *Through his children's book, Seuss warned of the dangers of cutting down too many trees.*

Many of the education efforts during this time were directed at children—a group almost completely ignored by earlier generations of environmentalists. The typical child of the early 1970s was exposed to a barrage of pro-environment messages. Since by this time nearly every American family had at least one television set, many of these messages were delivered over the air. "Give a Hoot— Don't Pollute!"[73] urged Woodsy Owl, a character created by the U.S. Forest Service, in public service announcements broadcast all across the country. Television cartoon shows during the period often had an environmentalist thrust, too. Many programs had characters reminding audiences not to litter. Others included songs with antipollution messages, such as the song "Mr. Factory" used on the 1970 cartoon show *Archie's Funhouse.*

Environmentalists also used more traditional means to educate children about

An Environmental Revolution ■ 57

their cause. In 1971, for example, best-selling children's author Dr. Seuss published *The Lorax*, a cautionary tale about the environmental dangers of cutting down too many trees. "Grow a forest," Seuss advised his readers in the book's text. "Protect it from axes that hack."[74] Nonfiction books about pollution and other environmental issues began to proliferate during this time as well. Some of these were evenhanded treatments of the issues, while others were more alarmist: "Will we end pollution before it kills us?"[75] asked a book published in 1967. Even the comic books of the period often discussed environmental problems. The Forest Service's Woodsy Owl got a comic series of his own in 1973, and storylines in long-running series such as Richie Rich and Donald Duck featured characters organizing community cleanups of playgrounds or urging corporate executives to stop polluting lakes and streams.

Environmental awareness made its way into schools as well. Teachers at all grade levels broadened science classes to include ecological issues. In many schools students explored local ponds and grasslands, observing and analyzing the ecosystems of their region. Students took part in simulations such as Man in His Environment, in which students played the roles of planners who had to make decisions about land use; they learned about the causes of pollution; they wrote letters to their senators and representatives requesting better protections for endangered animals. These programs were highly successful in raising awareness of the issues among

schoolchildren. Indeed, in 1973 government official William Ruckelshaus listed programs like these as among the most important environmental achievements of the previous few years.

The "Crying Indian," New Information, and Earth Day

Many pro-environment messages were aimed at adults, too. Among the most effective was a public service announcement sponsored by an environmental group called Keep America Beautiful. The announcement is remembered by many who saw it as the "crying Indian" commercial. It begins with a man in traditional Native American clothing paddling a canoe along a waterway. (Though viewers were expected to assume the man was Native American, the actor who portrayed him was actually of Italian descent.) It soon becomes clear that the water is full of litter and that its banks are lined with ugly, smoky factories. Later the man wanders along a highway, where a bag of garbage thrown by a driver lands at his feet. A tear begins trickling down the man's face as the announcer intones, "People start pollution. People can stop it."[76]

Environmentalists also wrote books aimed at adults to publicize the threat to the natural world. A book with the hopeful title *The Environment Can Be Saved* appeared in 1970; its author, Nelson Rockefeller, was a politician and a member of one of the wealthiest families in the United States. The following year a writer named Harry Caudill published a less optimistic discussion of strip mining, which was destroying mountaintops in Appalachian states like West Virginia and Tennessee. Caudill, who grew up in the strip-mining country of eastern Kentucky, titled his book *My Land Is Dying*. He warned that the mountain ecosystems of the region would soon be past repair if something was not done—and soon. Dozens of other books with environmental themes appeared during this period as well.

Educational campaigns took other forms, too. Activists publicized sobering statistics such as the number of years it takes for certain types of litter to decompose; aluminum cans, for example, may last for over a century. Towns devised catchy slogans to encourage citizens to pick up after themselves. And environmental advocates of this time publicized ecological disasters as never before. A 1969 oil spill off the coast of California devastated the population of seabirds and fouled beaches for hundreds of miles. Following the spill, activists began circulating pictures of filthy coastlines and oil-soaked ducks. The pictures showed clearly just how much harm humans could do to the world around them.

Thousands of people crowd Fifth Avenue in New York City on Earth Day. The celebration was established as a way to raise concern about the environment.

Pesticides and the Law

In 1967, several years after the publication of *Silent Spring*, a group of lawyers and environmentalists formed an organization called the Environmental Defense Fund. Over the next four years, this organization filed a number of lawsuits to try to get DDT banned. In 1971, in response to one of these suits, a federal court ordered the government to remove DDT from the list of allowable pesticides.

Companies that made DDT protested, however. After another year of debate, William Ruckelshaus, the head of the newly-formed Environmental Protection Agency, sided largely with the Environmental Defense Fund and agreed to ban nearly all uses of the chemical. Another year of suits and countersuits followed. In 1973, at last, another court ruled that Ruckelshaus had acted correctly. The case was settled, and DDT went almost entirely off the market.

Though DDT is hardly ever used nowadays, other pesticides continue to be manufactured. Farmers spray them on their fields; governments and homeowners use them for insect control. Environmentalists continue to worry about the effect of some of these toxins, however, and a few activists would like to ban most artificial pesticides altogether. The debate about controlling insect pests is by no means over.

A photograph shows many pesticides containing DDT available in the United States. In 1973 almost all products containing DDT went off the market.

The grandest educational effort of them all, however, was a celebration known as Earth Day. Planned and executed by an assortment of college students, political activists, and government leaders, the first Earth Day was observed in communities across the nation in April 1970. Author Mary Graham describes the celebration as "part seminar [college class], part carnival, and part environmental protest."[77] The main goal of Earth Day, however, was to alert people to the seriousness of the situation. "We are in an environmental crisis which threatens the survival of this nation,"[78] warned activist Barry Commoner in a journal article written to coincide with the first Earth Day.

These educational efforts had an impact on people's behavior. The anti-littering campaigns, for example, helped reduce the amount of roadside trash in many communities. Widely distributed photos of strip-mined mountaintops and oil-infested beaches convinced people that humans could indeed damage the health of the planet. Earth Day celebrations were effective, too; as one commentator wrote afterward, "Even the small children, who didn't know much about the cause . . . possibly will remember, for the rest of their lives, that picking up trash is the thing to do."[79] Perhaps most significant of all, a 1970 survey revealed that environmental protection was the second most important concern among Americans, trailing only crime. In a survey taken just five years earlier, hardly anyone had named the environment as a major issue. Where education was concerned, the activists had done their work—and done it well.

Another Strategy

The environmentalists of the Earth Day years knew that educating the public could only help their cause. At the same time they recognized that education would not be enough. Environmentally friendly policies helped the land—and ultimately, the people—but created burdens as well. "Clean air," editorialized a newspaper in 1971, "cannot be achieved without paying a price."[80] The same was true of clean water, wildlife protection, and a host of other goals. Sometimes the price to be paid was in setting limits on human activities. Protecting an endangered bird species, for example, meant staying away from its nesting grounds. And sometimes the cost was inconvenience and discomfort: Reducing the effects of pesticides, say, meant that more people would be bothered by flies and bitten by mosquitoes.

The most common cost, however, was financial. This burden was particularly apparent for manufacturers, which as a group were responsible for much of the nation's air and water pollution. Even in the late 1960s, the technology existed to treat liquid waste before factories released it into rivers, for example; similarly, special scrubbers could remove many of the harmful chemicals from factory smoke. These technologies, however, cost money. Factory owners were not eager to take on extra expenses, even in the interests of creating a cleaner world. Advocates for the environment believed that most manufacturers, if left to their own devices, would move very slowly to reduce pollution and that some might refuse to change their habits at all.

The same was true for ordinary citizens. At the time, for example, most gasolines contained lead, which helped engines run more smoothly. Once released into the atmosphere, however, the lead damaged the hearts, brains, and reproductive systems of animals and humans alike. Unleaded versions of gasoline were available, but they were more expensive than gasolines containing lead. While in theory many Americans of the time were eager to remove the lead from the gas they bought, the costs of doing so made some people think twice. As with the factories, some environmentalists feared that the added cost would cause many Americans to continue using the cheaper—if more toxic—leaded gas instead of switching to the less dangerous unleaded version.

The answer, activists decided, was to use the power of government by writing new laws that would mandate environmentally friendly actions on the part of businesses and the public alike. As one activist put it, "If we want them to do what is right, we must make them do what is right."[81] Accordingly, the environmentalists of the late 1960s and early 1970s spent much of their time lobbying for new laws. While they focused some of their attention on state and local governments, they concentrated mainly on making changes at the federal level. In this approach they were following the recent example of the civil rights movement, which had gotten the federal government to protect the rights of African Americans when individual states often would not. Sweeping legislation such as the Voting Rights Act of 1965, which secured the right of blacks to vote throughout the country, inspired the ecological advocates of the Earth Day era; they hoped to enact similar nationwide protections for the environment.

The federal strategy made sense for another reason, too. Passage of new environmental legislation proceeded at different speeds in different places, and quite often the actions of one state or town had very little effect until surrounding areas followed suit. To improve the water quality of Lake Michigan, for example, Illinois could forbid towns from dumping sewage directly into the lake—but the water would remain polluted unless neighboring Indiana did the same. Moreover, some factories had become adept at using the differences between state regulations to their benefit. If a state considered a new antipollution law, say, some of its factories might threaten to move to places where the laws were less stringent. Faced with possible job losses, the states often backed down. It was clear to environmentalists that only federal action—which would affect all states equally and at the same time—could bring about lasting environmental change.

New Legislation

Environmentalists began pushing for new federal laws well before Earth Day. One of the first of these, in fact, became law in 1964, well before most Americans had become concerned about the state of the environment. This legislation, known

A factory produces clouds of pollution. Environmental activists urged factory owners to take steps to reduce industrial waste.

as the Wilderness Act, extended extra protection to certain wilderness areas that were already part of the national forest or national park systems. Most of these areas were remote; the act lyrically defined "wilderness" as "an area where the earth and its community of life are untrammeled [undisturbed] by man, where man himself is a visitor who does not remain."[82] Perhaps most important, the act made it difficult to shrink the boundaries of these regions in the future. According to the new law, reducing the size of a wilderness area could not be done by a committee or a federal agency. Only another act of Congress could redraw the borders.

The Wilderness Act was a hint of things to come. The Water Quality Act of 1965, another federal law, went into effect the following year. This legislation required states to set standards of cleanliness in bodies of water that they shared with other states. Notably, the federal government reserved the right to set standards for states that did not set standards of their own. That same year Congress also passed the Highway Beautification Act, which set limits on the size, number, and type of billboards along many major roads and encouraged the planting of flowers and trees near American highways. "This bill will bring the wonders of nature back into our daily lives," said President Lyndon John-

Lady Bird Johnson plants flowers as a part of her mission to beautify America. Johnson was an influential force behind the Highway Beautification Act of 1965.

son, whose wife, Lady Bird Johnson, had been a strong force behind the new law. "[It] will enrich our spirits and restore a small measure of our national greatness."[83]

Then in 1969 the government went a step further by passing the National Environmental Policy Act. This bill required government agencies to take environmental issues into account when planning projects such as new highways or dams. This act, wrote its sponsors, sought to establish "a national policy which will encourage productive and enjoyable harmony between man and his environment."[84] Support for the bill was overwhelming. Of the 535 members of Congress, just 15 voted against the proposal.

Today it may seem unremarkable that government should be required to consider the environment when making decisions. At the time, however, the act represented a dramatic shift in the way Americans thought about the role of government—and the importance of the environment. Indeed, some historians consider the passage of the National Environmental Policy Act to be the first major success of the modern environmentalist movement.

Clean Air, Clean Water

The most important years of environmental legislation, however, began in 1970. That summer, soon after the first Earth Day celebration, President Richard Nixon issued an order that created a new federal bureau. Known as the Environmental Protection Agency, or EPA, this organization was responsible for fixing the damage done to the natural world—and was charged with preventing further harm to the planet. "We shall be an advocate for the environment with industry, with individuals, and within government," promised William Ruckelshaus, the agency's first director. "The ultimate goal of the EPA will be to encourage all Americans to adopt an environmentalist ethic."[85] With the establishment of the EPA, the federal government was putting its weight firmly behind environmental protection.

More laws quickly followed—and like the federal legislation that came out of the civil rights movement, many of these laws were far-reaching and powerful. The Clean Air Act of 1970 was one of the strongest. Under this law, the EPA singled out six substances that were commonly found in polluted air throughout the nation. These substances, which included lead, carbon monoxide, and soot, were chosen because they were known to affect human health. The EPA sharply limited the amounts of these substances that could be in the air. The government then tested air throughout the nation to see how many of these substances the air contained. If the air in a given community was over the limit for any of the six, it failed the test. The federal government could then require the state or local government to develop a plan to fix the problem.

The Clean Air Act did other things, too. For one, it set limits on the pollutants that could be added to the air by cars and trucks. For another, it set aside money for air pollution research. The effect of the law was gradual rather than immediate; it did not require companies and munic-

The Environmental Protection Agency, or EPA, in Washington, D.C., was established to prevent further environmental destruction.

ipalities to stop all toxic pollution at once, but instead allowed the problem to be fixed over time. Still, from its outset the law was a valuable tool for environmentalists. Though Congress had previously made some attempts to control air pollution (the 1970 law was actually an amendment to an earlier, largely ineffective measure), the Clean Air Act of 1970 represented an important step forward for the environmental movement.

The Clean Air Act was followed two years later by the Clean Water Act. This act did for water quality what the Clean Air Act had done for air. Its stated goal was "to restore and maintain the chemical, physical, and biological integrity of the nation's waters."[86] Under this law po-

tential polluters—such as manufacturers, city sewer systems, and power plants—needed a permit to dump waste into rivers, lakes, and oceans. If the pollutants in the waste caused serious damage to these waters, the government could require the polluters to install antipollution devices before renewing the permit. At the same time, the Clean Water Act made federal money available to communities to help them remodel water treatment plants in an effort to cut water pollution.

Like the Clean Air Act, the provisions of the Clean Water Act were phased in over a period of time. The lawmakers who wrote the act, however, were optimistic. By 1983, the new law read, all U.S.

waterways were to be clean enough to support aquatic life—and safe as well for people who wanted to use the water for recreation. The waters, in short, were to be "fishable and swimmable"[87] within a decade of the law's passage. Moreover, the Clean Water Act mandated that by 1985 no further discharges of any kind would be permitted into American waters. It was an ambitious timetable, and—as it turned out—an unworkable one. Still, for environmental activists, caught up as they were in the excitement of the movement's continuing success, these goals seemed realistic and necessary.

The Clean Air and Clean Water acts were revolutionary in another way as well. For most of U.S. history, in order to win a lawsuit, Americans have needed to show that they have been harmed by the person, government, or corporation they are suing. Traditionally, "harm" has meant physical injury or financial loss. The environmental legislation of the early 1970s, however, broadened the circumstances in which people could sue.

Land Use Controls

The environmental movement did not achieve all its goals during the early 1970s. One goal activists could not attain had to do with land use regulations. In 1970 Washington senator Henry Jackson introduced a bill to establish a national land use policy. According to Jackson, the proposed law would make sure that "*all* future development" would be "in harmony with sound scientific principles." State and local governments would determine the ecological needs of a given area and allow building in that area only if it did not interfere with those needs. These governments might forbid a developer from building houses in an area prone to flooding, for example, or require developers to set aside a percentage of land as open space when they built office complexes or shopping centers.

In 1972 the Senate approved a version of Jackson's original proposal; in early 1974 a House committee approved it as well. Later that year, though, several key supporters of the bill—including President Richard Nixon—changed their positions. Increasing opposition by building interests was certainly a factor; the cost of implementing the law may have been another. Whatever the reason, the bill did not pass the House as a whole. The land use bill was one of the few disappointments for environmentalists in the early 1970s.

Quoted in Adam Rome, *The Bulldozer in the Countryside.* New York: Cambridge University Press, 2001, p. 237.

In particular, the new laws specified that environmentalists—or environmentalist groups—could sue polluters on behalf of the public, even if the people bringing the lawsuit could not show that they had been directly harmed. Activists, therefore, could sue companies that polluted the air and water, and if the government was slow to enforce its new laws, then environmentalists could sue the government as well. This change provided the environmental movement with a new and important weapon.

One More Law

In 1973 Congress passed yet another landmark piece of legislation: the Endangered Species Act. Though several laws from the 1960s offered some protection to threatened animals and plants, environmentalists believed that these laws were inadequate. President Nixon, along with most members of Congress, agreed. Like the Clean Air and Clean Water acts, the Endangered Species Act of 1973 was quite broad. The new law sketched out a process for determining which plants and animals were endangered and then required the government to make plans to protect the threatened species.

The act was effective, but two features made it especially strong. The first had to do with habitat, or the homes of animals and plants. Without the proper habitat, species cannot thrive. Recognizing this, lawmakers wrote the Endangered Species Act so it protected not only the threatened species, but the species' habitat as well.

The other feature had to do with the basis for deciding whether a species should be listed as endangered or not. Some business owners did not want rare species to be protected if those species could be harvested and sold for a good profit. Timber companies, for example, fought to have several varieties of trees kept off the list, not because these species were plentiful—they were not—but because they represented an important source of the corporations' income. The Endangered Species Act, however, rejected the notion that economics should determine whether species appeared on the list. The act specified that the decision to list a species as endangered should be made "solely on the basis of the best scientific . . . data available"[88]—not because of commercial considerations.

By 1973, then, the environmental movement had reached a high point. Education and legislation had combined to raise public awareness of the problems facing the natural world—and had gone a long way toward fixing them. A steady stream of public service announcements, television shows with environmental themes, and pictures of ecological disasters had made *pollution* and *litter* household words. Thanks to the Clean Air and Clean Water acts, among others, broad environmental protections had been written into the law. In just a few years, the country had gone from limited, haphazard protection of its natural resources and its citizens' health to sweeping measures that made the environment a high priority. It was an amazing shift, and for the moment, at least, the environmental movement had carried the day.

Chapter Five

New Worries, New Approaches

In some ways the environmental activists of the early 1970s achieved a permanent victory. The environmental awareness that began in the 1960s and culminated a few years later is still present in American life. As writer Richard Louv puts it, "A kid today can likely tell you about the [ecology of the] Amazon rain forest"[89]—a subject of little importance to Americans just a generation or two ago. Present-day elementary school social studies and science textbooks, similarly, typically emphasize the need for Americans to protect the environment. And while some government leaders have tried to weaken the pro-environment laws of the 1970s, most of these laws are not only still in place in the twenty-first century, they have been expanded as well.

But environmentalists have not been able to rest easy. Though they have done excellent work in areas such as preservation of wilderness and regulation of air pollution—concerns that George Perkins

Marsh, Rachel Carson, and John Muir, among others, would have understood and appreciated—the scope of environmentalism has grown considerably since the early 1970s. Environmental activists today face problems that earlier advocates never dreamed of. As they try to solve these new concerns, modern-day environmentalists draw inspiration and tactics from earlier activists. They mix new ideas with old ones; they adapt the strategies of Theodore Roosevelt and Henry David Thoreau to the realities of the modern world. In this way the environmental movement connects seamlessly to the past, while at the same time looking forward to the future.

Backlash and Doubts

Although the environmental movement made some permanent strides in the early 1970s, it experienced some backlash in the years that followed. One reason was that the environmental movement of the early

President Richard Nixon stands on a beach in Key Biscayne, Florida. Nixon supported clean water, but thought the Clean Water Act was too costly and ignored other American priorities.

1970s was almost *too* successful. Garbage along roadsides and in vacant lots became much less of a problem as the decade wore on. Skies began to clear over U.S. cities that had formerly been blanketed by smog. Beaches reopened on long-polluted waterways. It seemed to many Americans that the environmental movement had met essentially all its goals. If true, placing continued focus on the health of the planet seemed unreasonable.

A second problem had to do with money. Environmental protection was

costly, and some of the new laws were extremely expensive. Congress set aside several billion dollars to implement and enforce the Clean Water Act alone. Legal costs, staffing, monitoring pollution levels—all cost money. Even by 1972 some politicians were concerned about the costs associated with environmental protection. President Richard Nixon had supported the Clean Air Act and believed that clean water was a worthy goal, for example, but he thought the costs of the Clean Water Act were simply too high. "We [must] attack pollution in a way that does not ignore other very real threats to the quality of life," Nixon explained, "such as spiraling prices and increasingly onerous [that is, burdensome] taxes."[90] The United States, he reminded Americans, had other priorities, too.

The money question soon became especially significant. The big environmental laws had been passed during a time of relative prosperity. Wages were rising, production of goods was on the upswing, and people generally felt good about the economy. By the mid-1970s, though, that was no longer the case. Now prices were shooting up quickly, while companies were cutting back on jobs and salaries were remaining stagnant. Given the economy, environmental protection struck some Americans as a luxury that they could not afford. "If you've got lots of people in the construction trades out of work," noted an environmentalist in 1975, "they're not going to be very fastidious [choosy] about where and how growth takes place."[91]

Property Rights

A third problem had to do with the tension between property rights and environmental protection. For years, with certain exceptions, American landowners had been entitled to do with their land more or less what they chose. The environmental legislation of the early 1970s, however, gave new authority to the government. No longer could property owners simply build a shopping center or housing complex on their land; now the government had the right to de-termine if the construction would increase the danger of flooding, contribute to water pollution, or reduce the habitat of an endangered species. If any of those applied, the government could—in theory, at least—stop the construction.

For some Americans, this was an alarming proposition. Under the new environmental laws, complained a U.S. representative, "all real property will be not owned, but merely 'held,' at the sufferance [by permission] of the State. Whatever the State thinks the landholder must do in the people's interest, he [the landholder] will be forced to do."[92] A coalition of like-minded people soon formed to oppose this notion—and other parts of the environmentalists' agenda as well. Farmers unhappy about rules against pesticides, ranchers angry because cattle-attacking wolves were now a protected species, developers frustrated by the environmental reviews the new laws called for—all came together beneath the banner of property rights.

Finally, and perhaps most important, the public perception of environmentalists began to change. Environmentalists had once seemed like knights in shining armor, engaged in a great battle to save America. By the middle of the 1970s, some Americans had come to believe that the environmental movement was against progress and out of touch with the needs of ordinary people: By demanding environmental reviews and pushing for manufacturers to pay for antipollution devices, environmental activists were out to destroy businesses and deny people jobs. "Those [']stop everything['] environmentalists are the cause of much of our country's unemployment,"[93] an angry Montana man wrote in a letter to his local newspaper. The expense of meeting new environmental standards, he claimed, had forced the company he owned out of business.

The Snail Darter

In 1975 a well-publicized incident in Tennessee fueled the growing hostility toward environmentalism. At the time, a government agency called the Tennessee Valley Authority had begun building a new dam along the Little Tennessee River. The dam seemed to make perfect sense. The region was economically depressed, so its construction provided nearby workers with badly needed jobs. The risk of flooding in the region would be much reduced once the dam was in place. And the dam would generate electricity—enough, reported one commentator, to meet the needs of thirty thousand people every day. There seemed no reason to oppose the construction of the dam—and many reasons to support it.

A small fish called the snail darter, however, lived in the river near the dam site. The snail darter was an endangered species, and it seemed apparent that building the dam would be harmful to this population—and possibly make the fish extinct. Activists immediately tried to stop construction on the dam. The law was on their side. The Endangered Species Act of 1973 specifically barred activities—such as the building of a dam—that would damage the habitat of an already-threatened species. And of course these protections were in place even if a project carried important economic benefits, such as jobs or more widely available electricity. According to the act, halting construction was the only possible course of action.

Tennessee Valley Authority officials objected, however, and the case soon wound up in court. The environmentalists quickly discovered that even if they had the law on their side, public opinion was against them. Many observers were scandalized that the activists would support the survival of a small fish over the benefits the dam provided. "The 1,500 snail darters, on [environmentalists'] scale of values," wrote columnist Rus Walton, "are more important than flood-control, power, and jobs." Walton suggested that if environmentalists were so eager to save the snail darter, they should personally pay back the money the government had already spent on the dam's construction. "It's time these folks started paying for the consequences of their actions," Walton wrote. "That might begin to balance hysteria with a little common sense."[94] The environmentalists' campaign to save the snail darter had turned into a public relations disaster.

Through the Reagan Years

By the early 1980s the environmental movement had reached a low point. Ronald Reagan, who was elected president in 1980, did very little to stop polluters or extend protections to wildlife, particularly during his first term. Reagan's first head of the EPA, Anne Gorsuch, cut the EPA's budget by over 20 percent immediately upon assuming office and tried to weaken earlier legislation by permitting higher levels of pollutants in the air and water. Reagan's secretary of the interior, James Watt, was even more combative: He called environmentalists "the greatest threat to the ecology of the West" and charged that their ultimate goal was to "bring down the type of government I believe in."[95] It had been years since environmentalists were so thoroughly excluded from power.

Even through these troubles, though, the environmental movement remained an important force in American life and politics. Though Americans did not always approve of the environmentalists' methods and priorities, most still agreed with the basic goals of the movement. No one wanted to return to the days of choking smog and oil-slicked rivers. And while few Americans cared much about the fate of the snail darter, there was considerably more support for protection of larger, more familiar species such as wolves, grizzly bears, and eagles. Indeed, some studies showed that the Reagan administration's opposition to the environmentalists actually increased support for many of the activists' objectives. The backlash against environmentalism had now produced a backlash of its own.

The environmentalist movement had several successes during this period, too.

An EPA sign on the Roebling Steel site declares it as a part of the Superfund project. The project dealt with toxic waste and sites where hazardous materials were dumped.

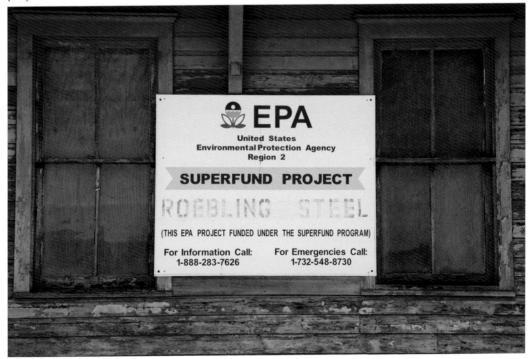

"It Was Making Us Sick"

In the early 1980s a waste treatment plant known as the Rollins Environmental Services Facility was built near Alsen, Louisiana, a relatively poor and all-black community not far from Baton Rouge. The construction of the plant changed life for the people of the town, as community activist Mary McCastle describes:

We had no warning Rollins was coming in here. When they did come in we didn't know what they were dumping. We did know that it was making us sick. People used to have nice gardens and fruit trees. They lived off their gardens and only had to buy meat. Some of us raised hogs and chickens. But not after Rollins came in. Our gardens and animals were dying out. Some days the odors from the plant would be nearly unbearable. We didn't know what was causing it. We later found out that Rollins was burning hazardous waste.

Quoted in Bill McKibben, ed., *American Earth: Environmental Writing Since Thoreau.* New York: Library of America, 2008, pp. 733–34.

Perhaps the most important of these was a law known as Superfund, passed by Congress in 1980. Superfund dealt with toxic waste sites—places where chemicals and other hazardous materials had been dumped. The law allowed the government to force those responsible for polluting these sites to clean them up. If the responsible parties could not be found, the law set aside money for the federal government to do the cleaning itself. The need for Superfund became apparent after people began getting sick in places where toxic chemicals had been deposited, such as the Love Canal neighborhood of Niagara Falls, New York.

Environmentalists also prevailed in other battles. In 1976, for example, Congress passed a law protecting whales in American waters. Two years later, the National Energy Act offered incentives for people and businesses to use fuel more efficiently. Pressure from activists and other concerned citizens led Ronald Reagan to increase the EPA's budget during his second term; in 1985 he also added millions of acres of wilderness to the list of federally protected lands. And in 1990 a large majority of representatives and senators from both parties supported a new addition to the Clean Air Act, which called for strict new limitations on vehicle emissions into the atmosphere.

Recycling, Education, and Corporate America

Since 1990 the environmentalist movement has continued to have its ups and downs. On the positive side, surveys consistently show that a majority of Americans support environmental protection. Earth Day celebrations continue each year, though they are not as well attended as they were in the early 1970s. The laws protecting endangered species remain generally strong. Auto emissions are down from what they were, some of the most badly polluted rivers and landfills have been cleaned up, and the environmental disasters of earlier times, such as the smog that covered Donora in 1948 or the burning of the Cuyahoga River in 1969, have not been repeated.

Recycling has been another achievement. Until relatively recently, materials such as paper, cans, and bottles ended up in dumps or were burned in incinerators; either way they caused pollution and wasted important resources. Today, however, recycling programs are common. Most cities and towns offer curbside pickup of paper, cardboard, plastic containers, and other materials. Environmentalists of the twenty-first century still push to increase the rate at which people recycle, but they have succeeded in establishing recycling as a part of ordinary life.

Educational efforts continue, too. Echoing the efforts of the early 1970s, twenty-first century comic books, television shows, and public service announcements frequently urge Americans to

Children fill a recycling bin with reusable materials. Recycling programs have become common in recent years.

The Spotted Owl Controversy

A bird called the northern spotted owl was at the center of an environmental controversy in the late twentieth century. The spotted owl lived in the forests of the Pacific Northwest—in trees that were frequently cut down by loggers. In 1973, when the Endangered Species Act went into effect, however, the owl's population was still too large to qualify it for protection under the law.

Over time, though, the spotted owl became rarer. To protect the owl, environmental activists advocated a ban on logging near owl populations. Lumber companies, in turn, warned of bankruptcy if they were kept from these areas. The region's people, many of whom relied on logging for their livelihoods, argued against protecting the owls. "Save a logger," argued one bumper sticker; "eat a spotted owl." But the activists carried the day: In the early 1990s much of the forest was placed off-limits to loggers.

Both sides of the debate found the owl to be a powerful symbol for their perspective. To some, the owl represented all that was good about environmentalism—and to others, all that was troublesome about it. Even today the spotted owl remains an important symbol for environmentalism, both pro and con.

Quoted in Wayne Lynch, *Owls of the United States and Canada.* Baltimore: Johns Hopkins University, 2007, p. 205.

Environmental activists protected the northern spotted owl species by supporting a ban on logging near owl populations.

adopt a "greener"—that is, more environmentally friendly—outlook on life. Indeed, American companies of today strive to associate themselves with environmental awareness. Corporations advertise their organic foods or their energy-efficient appliances in hopes of attracting customers. Johnson Controls, a manufacturer of car interiors, uses the slogan "a more comfortable, safe, and sustainable world,"[96] and logging company Weyerhaeuser says that it "grow[s] trees in a socially and environmentally responsible manner."[97]

New Challenges

At the same time, threats to the environment have become more complex and harder to resolve. "Pollution today is greatly changed from the 1970s," says a fisherman. "Then we saw the problem as a bunch of big polluters. We could see, smell and touch the ugly green beds of algae floating on the Potomac River." Today, in contrast, much water pollution comes from farms, gasoline engines, and other relatively small sources, which makes it more difficult to regulate; and much of the danger it presents is from chemicals that are invisible. "The water looks OK," sums up the fisherman, "but science tells us it is not."[98]

Nor is pollution the only—or even the most important—threat facing the environment today. Ecological issues today include problems that George Perkins Marsh and Theodore Roosevelt knew nothing about. Energy is a good example. Most traditional sources of energy are not environmentally friendly. Coal

mines damage the countryside. Oil spills when it is being transported. Moreover, coal, oil, and natural gas are not renewable; that is, the world has a limited supply of these fuels. Environmentalists today advocate the development of renewable fuels, such as wind power and solar energy, that cause less damage to the environment. Though renewable sources make up only a small part of America's energy consumption, that proportion is rising.

Another example of a new debate is the environmental justice movement. As pollution has become less acceptable to Americans, dirty air, dirty water, and other forms of contamination are getting harder to find in white middle-class neighborhoods—but remain common in areas where poor people and minorities live. Many observers believe that this is no coincidence. Historically, racial minorities and poor people have struggled to make their voices heard in politics and government. Until well into the 1800s, poor people were barred from voting in many places, and laws and customs in parts of the country kept blacks from the polls through the middle of the twentieth century.

Today, the barriers to participation in government are not as high, but difficulties remain. Perhaps most notably, political leaders are often quite responsive to money: political campaigns are costly, and wealthy backers can do a great deal to influence an election. Indeed, political candidates spend a great deal of time fundraising—and, some would charge, making sure that they vote in a way that suits their wealthy constituents. Well-off Americans can thus buy access to their lawmakers in a way that the poor cannot.

This lack of political power in poor and minority neighborhoods, some observers charge, is the reason why these neighborhoods have so many environmental hazards. Governments and businesses, these people assert, target poor and minority areas for dumps, waste treatment plants, and polluting oil refineries. If these plants were built in well-to-do areas, local citizens would complain bitterly to their representatives and pool their resources to change the situation. Poorer residents, in contrast, may have a more difficult time organizing themselves—and certainly have a more difficult time making their case heard.

When a company installed a hazardous waste site near Alsen, Louisiana, for example, residents complained to no avail; often residents of poor neighborhoods do not have the political power to change the situation. "Alsen is black and a nowhere place stuck out in the parish [county]," notes one activist, explaining why no one outside the town paid much attention. "It didn't count."[99] Many of today's environmentalists hope to ensure that all Americans, regardless of income or race, are protected from pollution and other environmental hazards.

Climate Change

The most significant new environmental issue, though, is the problem of climate change. As early as the mid-1800s, George Perkins Marsh had noted that by clearing forests and burning fuels, humans had increased the average temperature in parts of the Mediterranean Sea. By the 1980s evidence suggested that temperatures were rising across the globe—and that so-called greenhouse gases, produced by the burning of coal, oil, and other fuels, were a significant reason why. This phenomenon, sometimes known as global warming, is more accurately called anthropogenic climate change. This phrase refers to long-term changes in the weather—caused partly or mostly by people.

The extent of climate change is debatable, and the degree to which humanity contributes to it is also unclear. Nearly all scientists who study the issue, however, agree that temperatures in most parts of the planet have risen in recent years; that storms and other types of severe weather seem to be on the increase; and that human activities play an important role in the changes. Climate change, especially if it proceeds rapidly, could cause chaos for many animal and plant species. The polar bear, for example, lives in the Arctic, which is heating up considerably. The heat melts the ice that the bear uses to hunt and raise its cubs. "With its sea ice domain melting ever sooner and farther by the season," writes scientist William Stolzenburg, "the polar bear's home may be nearly gone within fifty years."[100]

Climate change will also affect people. As temperatures rise rainfall may decrease rapidly in parts of the world, turning extensive stretches of currently fertile land into desert. Melting ice in Greenland and Antarctica may raise ocean levels across the globe, possibly flooding coastal cities

A polar bear hesitantly tests the stability of moving ice. Arctic wildlife could be in danger due to climate changes and increasing temperatures.

such as Boston and Miami. Air pollution tends to go up as temperatures increase, which would worsen pollution-related health problems. Warmer temperatures are more favorable for the spread of mosquitoes, so diseases that mosquitoes carry may become more common. "Climate change," summarizes a 2004 EPA memo, "has global consequences for human health."[101]

Given the threat climate change presents to the natural world and to human beings, environmentalists have recently made global warming an extremely high priority. To fight against it they have used many of the same tactics that earlier envi-

ronmental advocates pioneered. Education is one. Just as children of the 1970s grew up surrounded by antipollution messages, children of the early 2000s are well aware of the problems of global warming. While many of these efforts are aimed at children, others focus primarily on adults. Former vice president Al Gore, for example, has devoted much of his career in and out of politics to spreading warnings about the danger of climate change.

Scientific advocacy is another strategy. Just as Rachel Carson cited research to demonstrate the dangers of pesticides in the 1960s, scientists of the twenty-first century are gathering data and running

Al Gore on the Environment

Former vice president Al Gore is one of the best-known voices for the environmentalist cause. In this excerpt from an interview, Gore likens the environmental movement to the earlier battle against Soviet-style Communism during the 1940s through the 1980s.

The first step internationally is to make the effort to save the earth's environment the central organizing principle for the post–Cold War world, just as we bent every effort to defeat Communism. Now, on a global basis, we have to develop this shared commitment to bend every effort toward saving the earth's environment. That sounds and seems impossible to many right now, just as a few years ago it seemed impossible to expect the Soviet Union to disappear and all of Eastern Europe to be free and democratic and capitalist. But when enough people change their way of thinking about communism, then what seemed impossible became imperative. Now as more and more people are changing their way of thinking about the earth's environment . . . what seems impossible will become imperative.

Quoted in Joseph Kaufman, ed. *The World According to Al Gore*. Los Angeles: Renaissance, 1999, pp. 109–10.

simulations to show the alarming effects of climate change. And just as Theodore Roosevelt and Henry David Thoreau had argued that nature had a right to exist, so too do activists of the early 2000s encourage Americans to develop a feeling of protectiveness toward nature. "We're headed into [a] mass extinction,"[102] warns one environmentalist, predicting that up to a quarter of all existing species may vanish if climate change is not stopped.

Global Warming and the Law

The most significant tactic, though, is the one used most effectively by the environmental movement of the early 1970s—the law. Laws to reduce the threat of climate change will have a major impact on the way Americans live their lives. Vehicle exhaust, for example, pumps tons of greenhouse gases into the atmosphere every year. To reduce this amount Americans may need to drive less, drive more energy-efficient vehicles, use alternative fuels that cause less pollution—or all three. Each approach has its drawbacks, however, most notably cost and convenience. Rather than expecting Americans to adopt these options on their own, therefore, environmentalists hope to pass legislation that will push the country closer to the goal of reducing emissions.

The proposed laws work in different ways. Some provide incentives for people to act in an environmentally friendly way. Americans who use alternative fuels, for instance, can qualify for tax breaks. Others follow the lead of the Clean Air Act and other legislation of the 1970s; they set standards and then mandate that companies reach them. One 2009 proposal, for example, called for automobile makers to build cars that can go 35.5 miles per gallon (15 km per L) by 2016, with emissions being lowered at the same time. Similar laws would require the manufacture of more energy-efficient lightbulbs, air conditioners, and other appliances.

Perhaps the most creative laws, though, are the cap-and-trade policies backed by President Barack Obama and many other government leaders. These laws would set a limit—a cap—on the amount of greenhouse gases that companies could emit into the atmosphere in a given year. The government would issue so-called carbon credits—essentially, licenses to pollute—to American companies. Each company would get a certain number of these credits. Companies could then buy and sell credits. A company that exceeds its limits for the year

E85 ethanol gas is an alternative fuel that can help reduce the amount of greenhouse gases caused by vehicle exhaust.

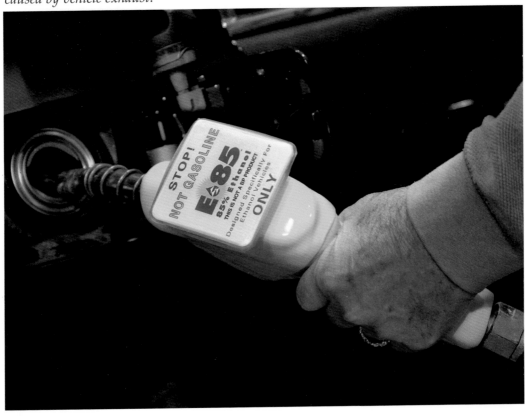

Radical Environmentalists

In recent years several groups of environmentalists have become increasingly radical in their support for the planet. Some regularly put themselves at great risk of injury or even death in their eagerness to protect the natural world. Members of the international advocacy group Greenpeace, for example, have gone out into the world's oceans in small boats and disrupted much larger ships hunting for whales.

In 1997, similarly, a woman named Julia Butterfly Hill climbed a California redwood to protest the logging of these enormous trees. Hill built a platform in the tree and made it her home, obtaining supplies from supporters on the ground. Other activists joined her at various times. Hill and the other activists believed that the lumber companies would not dare to cut down a tree in which people were living. As environmentalist and author Bill McKibben writes, "That turned out to be, just barely, true, though only after Hill had endured . . . helicopter attacks and attempts to cut off her supply of food." In the end Hill remained in the redwood for nearly two years before winning a promise from the lumber company not to touch that group of trees.

Bill McKibben, ed., *American Earth: Environmental Writing Since Thoreau.* New York: Library of America, 2008, p. 907.

Activist Julia Butterfly Hill sits in a California redwood to protest the logging of redwood trees.

could buy credits from other corporations, invest in antipollution equipment to keep its greenhouse gas emissions under the limit, or reduce production. The choice would be the company's, but the effect on the climate would be the same.

Not all the proposed laws are restricted to the United States; climate change is a worldwide problem. In 1997 a group of nations approved a treaty, or an international agreement, called the Kyoto Protocol. Countries that signed the treaty agreed to cut their production of greenhouse gases by a certain amount. Most countries have accepted the Kyoto Protocol, but as of early 2009 the United States was not among them. Environmentalists generally support the treaty, however, and continue to push the federal government to accept it.

Whether global warming can be stopped remains to be seen. Even the most optimistic researchers and observers recognize that the United States will need to make significant changes if this war against climate change is to be won. "We need better technologies,"[103] admits Steven Chu, Obama's secretary of energy. Still, though the stakes are high, in one sense the battle against climate change is not much different from the struggle to save the wilderness areas of the West, the fight to ban DDT, or the debate over the Clean Water Act. In each of these cases, the odds seemed against the environmental movement. Expenses, traditions, and at times even the law argued against the environmentalists' goals, and it often appeared unlikely that Yosemite would ever be protected, or that the skies over Donora would eventually be clear. Yet through hard work and a grab bag of strategies, the environmentalists prevailed in each of these battles. If history is any guide, they may be able to do the same for climate change.

Environmentalism and History

The impact of the environmental movement on the United States and on American history has been enormous. Naturalist and author Scott Weidensaul notes that as recently as 1953, "you could, with almost complete impunity, foul the air or waters, poison grizzlies, kill a jaguar, shoot hawks and owls, clear-cut millennia-old forests on public land, harpoon great whales for profit, traffic in rare species, spray any pesticide on the market (and market whatever you could concoct), or build dams to flood priceless canyons."[104] Today most of these activities are forbidden, and the others are regulated or viewed as much less acceptable. The construction of a new road, the disposal of a factory's waste, the filling in of a wetland—all are subject to the strictures of the legal system, a system which today includes protection for the natural world. Only a few decades ago, the needs of the environment, legally speaking, could be ignored. Now, in the twenty-first century, they must be taken into consideration. That has been a remarkable change.

Moreover, the expectations of Americans have evolved. Once, the people of the United States accepted environmental degradation as a natural part of economic progress. A factory that belched poisonous gases into the atmosphere during the 1870s, 1920s, or 1950s might be killing birds, might be fouling the air hundreds of miles away, might even be making people sick, but for many Americans these seemed to be trivial concerns. Pollution or no, the factory offered jobs, produced important goods, and embodied the greatness of American manufacturing. Next to that greater good, the well-being of the environment simply did not matter.

For the most part, though, Americans hold a different expectation today. In ways that earlier generations did not, the people of the twenty-first century recognize the complexity of the natural world and its connection with humanity. Environmentalism may not always win out, but it is always a part of the discussion. In 1900 or 1950 the destruction of a forest or the introduction of a new insecticide sparked little if any unease about the effect on animal species, groundwater supplies, or human life; today, in contrast, Americans often feel not just a legal obligation to consider the impact of their actions on nature, but a moral obligation to do so as well.

The greatest achievement of the environmental movement in America, then, is not necessarily any particular piece of legislation or group of policies, not the protection of Yellowstone or the passage of the Clean Water Act. Instead, it is a mind-set. In a remarkably short period of time, environmental awareness has gone from the fringes of American thought to the center of American life and political debate. The environmentalists of the past, along with the ecologists of today, have changed the way we act toward the world around us. But perhaps more importantly, they have changed forever the way we think about it.

Notes

Introduction: America and the Environment

1. Richard Louv, *Last Child in the Woods*. New York: Algonquin, 2008, p. 2.
2. Aldo Leopold, *A Sand County Almanac and Sketches Here and There*. 1949. Reprint, New York: Oxford University Press, 1970, pp. 224–25.

Chapter One: The Roots of Environmentalism

3. Leopold, *A Sand County Almanac*, p. vii.
4. Quoted in Alan Taylor and Eric Foner, *The American Colonies*. New York: Penguin, 2002, p. 131.
5. William Wood, *New England's Prospect*. Amherst: University of Massachusetts Press, 1977, p. 34.
6. Quoted in Ivan T. Sanderson, "A-h-h B-l-o-o-w-s," *American Heritage*, December 1960. www.americanheritage.com/articles/magazine/ah/1960/1/1960_1_48.shtml.
7. Quoted in John Franklin Jameson, *Narratives of New Netherland, 1609–1664*. New York: Charles Scribner's Sons, 1909, pp. 26–27.
8. Quoted in Jameson, *Narratives of New Netherland, 1609–1664*, p. 17.
9. John Josselyn, *New-England's Rarities Discovered*. Ann Arbor: University of Michigan Library, 2006, p. 59.
10. Quoted in Lee A. Vedder, *John James Audubon and The Birds of America*. San Marino, CA: Huntington Library, 2006, pp. 5–6.
11. Quoted in Michael P. Branch, *Reading the Roots*. Athens: University of Georgia Press, 2003, p. 187.
12. Quoted in Franklin G. Burroughs–Simeon B. Chapin Art Museum, "John James Audubon: American Artist and Naturalist," Myrtle Beach Art Museum. www.myrtlebeachartmuseum.org/museum_exhibit_19.htm.
13. Quoted in Frederick Doveton Nichols and Ralph E. Griswold, *Thomas Jefferson, Landscape Architect*. Charlottesville: University of Virginia Press, 2003, p. 32.
14. Quoted in Bill McKibben, ed., *American Earth: Environmental Writing Since Thoreau*. New York: Library of America, 2008, p. 41.
15. Quoted in McKibben, *American Earth*, p. 41.
16. Quoted in McKibben, *American Earth*, p. 42.
17. Quoted in William Stolzenburg, *Where the Wild Things Were*. New York: Bloomsbury, 2008, p. 172.
18. Quoted in Nichols and Griswold, *Thomas Jefferson, Landscape Architect*, p. 32.
19. Quoted in McKibben, *American Earth*, p. 31.
20. Quoted in McKibben, *American Earth*, p. 8.

21. Thoreau Farm Trust, "Thoreau Farm Trust Seeks Donations to Finish Thoreau Birthplace Restoration." www.thoreaufarm.org.
22. Quoted in McKibben, *American Earth*, p. 72.
23. McKibben, *American Earth*, p. 71.
24. Alexis de Tocqueville, *Democracy in America*, trans. Arthur Goldhammer. 1840. Reprint, New York: Library of America, 2004, p. 557.

Chapter Two: The Conservation Movement
25. Quoted in McKibben, *American Earth*, p. 103.
26. John James Audubon, "The Passenger Pigeon," National Audubon Society. www.audubon.org/bird/boa/F29_G3a.html.
27. Quoted in Thomas B. Allen, *Vanishing Wildlife of North America*. Washington, DC: National Geographic, 1974, p. 24.
28. Board of Regents of the Smithsonian Institution, *Report of the United States National Museum, 1887*. Washington, DC: Smithsonian Institution, 1887, p. 465.
29. *Bismarck* (ND) *Tribune*, "Scientific Wonders," November 25, 1881, p. 1.
30. Board of Regents of the Smithsonian Institution, *Report of the United States National Museum, 1887*, p. 465.
31. Quoted in John F. Sears, *Sacred Places*. New York: Oxford University Press, 1989, p. 38.
32. Quoted in Sears, *Sacred Places*, p. 163.
33. George A. Crofutt, *Crofutt's Transcontinental Tourist's Guide, Third Annual Revision*, University of Virginia Library. http://etext.virginia.edu/railton/roughingit/map/yoscrof.html.
34. Quoted in Sears, *Sacred Places*, p. 130.
35. Frederick Schwatka, "The Yellowstone Park," *New York Times*, July 5, 1886, p. 5.
36. Quoted in Sears, *Sacred Places*, p. 169.
37. Quoted in Tom Melham, *John Muir's Wild America*. Washington, DC: National Geographic, 1976, pp. 14–15.
38. Quoted in Melham, *John Muir's Wild America*, p. 72.
39. Quoted in Melham, *John Muir's Wild America*, p. 166.
40. Quoted in *Atlanta Constitution*, "Big Trees of the Sierra," August 24, 1890, p. 3.
41. Quoted in McKibben, *American Earth*, p. 109.
42. Quoted in Melham, *John Muir's Wild America*, p. 167.
43. Quoted in William O. Douglas, "John Muir's Public Service," Sierra Club. www.sierraclub.org/john_muir_exhibit/frameindex.html?http://www.sierraclub.org/john_muir_exhibit/life/john_muirs_public_service_by_william_o_douglas.html.
44. Quoted in Edmund Morris, *Theodore Rex*. New York: Random House, 2001, pp. 32–33.
45. Quoted in McKibben, *American Earth*, p. 130.
46. Quoted in McKibben, *American Earth*, p. 133.
47. Quoted in Morris, *Theodore Rex*, p. 519.
48. Quoted in McKibben, *American Earth*, p. 133.
49. Quoted in Gretel Ehrlich, *John Muir: Nature's Visionary*. Washington, DC: National Geographic, 2000, p. 212.
50. Quoted in Melham, *John Muir's Wild America*, p. 186.

Chapter Three: Science and the Environment

51. Quoted in Donald Worster, *A Passion for Nature*. New York: Oxford University Press, 2008, p. 161.
52. Quoted in National Park Service, "Theodore Roosevelt and Conservation." www.nps.gov/thro/history culture/theodore-roosevelt-and-con servation.htm.
53. Bob Beard, "20 Years Away from Colonizing Mars, Is Willy Ley's Opinion," *Greeley (CO) Daily Tribune*, February 12, 1960, p. 5.
54. Bill Clinton, "Remarks by the President at Clean Car Event," Environmental Protection Agency, December 21, 1999. www.epa.gov/history/top ics/caa90/14.htm.
55. Quoted in McKibben, *American Earth*, p. 304.
56. Quoted in McKibben, *American Earth*, p. 311.
57. *Monessen (PA) Daily Independent*, "A Blight on the Valley," November 2, 1948, p. 5.
58. *Waterloo (IA) Daily Courier*, "Poisonous Smog," November 2, 1948, p. 6.
59. Leopold, *A Sand County Almanac*, p. 198.
60. Quoted in Allan R. Talbot, *Power Along the Hudson*. New York: E.P. Dutton, 1972, p. 2.
61. Quoted in Adam Rome, *The Bulldozer in the Countryside*. New York: Cambridge University Press, 2001, p. 162.
62. Quoted in Thomas R. Dunlap, ed., *DDT*, Silent Spring, *and the Rise of Environmentalism*. Seattle: University of Washington Press, 2008, p. 41.
63. Quoted in Dunlap, *DDT*, Silent Spring, *and the Rise of Environmentalism*, p. 47.
64. Quoted in Dunlap, *DDT*, Silent Spring, *and the Rise of Environmentalism*, p. 54.
65. Quoted in McKibben, *American Earth*, p. 367.
66. Quoted in McKibben, *American Earth*, p. 375.
67. Quoted in Dunlap, *DDT*, Silent Spring, *and the Rise of Environmentalism*, p. 120.
68. *Anderson (IN) Daily Bulletin*, "DDT in the Antarctic," July 20, 1965, p. 4.
69. Quoted in Dunlap, *DDT*, Silent Spring, *and the Rise of Environmentalism*, p. 103.
70. Quoted in Rome, *The Bulldozer in the Countryside*, p. 109.

Chapter Four: An Environmental Revolution

71. Quoted in Mary Graham, *The Morning After Earth Day*. Washington, DC: Brookings Institution, 1999, p. 2.
72. Scott Weidensaul, *Return to Wild America*. New York: North Point, 2005, p. xvi.
73. Quoted in Don Markstein's Toonopedia, "Woodsy Owl." www.toonope dia.com/woodsy.htm.
74. Quoted in *Time*, "American Notes: California," October 2, 1989. www .time.com/time/magazine/article/0, 9171,958654,00.html?iid=chix-sphere.
75. Lucy Kavaler, *Dangerous Air*. New York: Day, 1967, front cover.
76. Quoted in Ad Council, "Pollution: Keep America Beautiful—Iron Eyes Cody." www.adcouncil.org/default .aspx?id=132.
77. Graham, *The Morning After Earth Day*, p. 1.
78. Quoted in Ronald Bailey, "Earth Day, Then and Now," *Reason*, May 2000.

www.reason.com/news/show/27702 .html.

79. Blonnie Pittman, "About That Earth Day," *Gastonia* (NC) *Gazette*, April 26, 1970, p. 19.

80. *Idaho Free Press*, "Clean Air Bill," January 1, 1971, p. 4.

81. Quoted in McKibben, *American Earth*, p. 482.

82. "The Wilderness Act of 1964," Wilderness.net. www.wilderness.net/ index.cfm?fuse=NWPS&sec=legisAct.

83. Quoted in McKibben, *American Earth*, p. 397.

84. "National Environmental Policy," U.S. Government Printing Office. http://frwebgate.access.gpo.gov/c gi-bin/getdoc.cgi?dbname=browse _usc&docid=Cite:+42USC4321.

85. William Ruckelshaus, "Environment Agency to Help," *Albuquerque Journal*, January 4, 1971, p. 4.

86. Quoted in Rome, *The Bulldozer in the Countryside*, pp. 110–11.

87. Quoted in Chris Carrel, "A New Legal Strategy Reinvigorates an Old Law," *Sierra*, May 1999. http://find articles.com/p/articles/mi_m1525/ is_3_84/ai_54492555.

88. Quoted in Tony A. Sullins, *ESA: Endangered Species Act*. Chicago: ABA, 2001, p. 13.

Chapter Five: New Worries, New Approaches

89. Louv, *Last Child in the Woods*, p. 1.

90. Quoted in Robert W. Adler, Jessica C. Landman, and Diane M. Cameron, *The Clean Water Act 20 Years Later*. Washington, DC: Island, 1993, p. 1.

91. Quoted in Rome, *The Bulldozer in the Countryside*, p. 248.

92. Quoted in Rome, *The Bulldozer in the Countryside*, p. 243.

93. Earl C. Clopton, "Environmental Types Are Destructive," *Montana Standard*, March 10, 1975, p. 4.

94. Rus Walton, "Fishy Scales," *Piqua* (OH) *Daily Call*, November 8, 1975, p. 3.

95. Quoted in Gil Troy, *Morning in America*. Princeton, NJ: Princeton University Press, 2007, p. 141.

96. Quoted in *Environmental Leader*, "Johnson Controls Refreshes Corporate Identity," October 1, 2007. www.environmentalleader.com/200 7/10/01/johnson-controls-refreshes-corporate-identity.

97. Weyerhaeuser.com, "Sustainability." www.weyerhaeuser.com/Sustainabi lity.

98. Hedrick Smith, "I Had No Idea What I Was Getting Into," *Frontline*, PBS. www.pbs.org/wgbh/pages/frontline /poisonedwaters/etc/notebook.html.

99. Quoted in McKibben, *American Earth*, p. 734.

100. Stolzenburg, *Where the Wild Things Were*, p. 214.

101. Quoted in Daniel J. Weiss and Robin Pam, "The Human Side of Global Warming," Center for American Progress, April 10, 2008. www .americanprogress.org/issues/ 2008/04/human_side.html.

102. Quoted in McKibben, *American Earth*, p. 877.

103. Quoted in Fareed Zakaria, "In the Great Ship *Titanic*," *Newsweek*, April 20, 2009. www.newsweek.com/id/ 193488/page/2.

104. Weidensaul, *Return to Wild America*, p. 350.

For Further Reading

Books

Rick Adair, ed., *Critical Perspectives on Politics and the Environment*. New York: Rosen, 2007. Articles and commentary on environmental issues such as energy use and endangered species.

William Dudley, *The Environment: Opposing Viewpoints*. San Diego: Greenhaven, 2001. Articles and arguments about environmental issues ranging from recycling and nuclear energy to pollution control. Includes commentary and guiding questions.

Gretel Ehrlich, *John Muir: Nature's Visionary*. Washington, DC: National Geographic, 2000. A beautifully illustrated book about Muir, quoting extensively from his writings.

J.S. Kidd and Renee A. Kidd, *Agriculture Versus Environmental Science*. New York: Facts On File, 2005. Explores the tension between farming and environmentalism, explaining how the two can be reconciled to create a more eco-friendly agricultural policy.

Aldo Leopold, *A Sand County Almanac and Sketches Here and There*. 1949. Reprint, New York: Oxford University Press, 1970. Leopold was a naturalist who studied the ecosystems around his home in great detail and wrote about his findings. He also wrote about the impact of human beings on nature at a time when few were much concerned about this issue.

Bill McKibben, ed., *American Earth: Environmental Writing Since Thoreau*. New York: Library of America, 2008. This long compilation of dozens of pieces about the environment is a good sourcebook.

Lawrence Pringle, *The Environmental Movement*. New York: HarperCollins, 2000. A fine overview of environmentalism with a focus on recent issues. Well written and well researched.

William Stolzenburg, *Where the Wild Things Were*. New York: Bloomsbury, 2008. About extinctions and scientists' attempts, now and in the past, to save large predators from dying out.

Jeca Taudte, *Our Planet: Change Is Possible*. New York: HarperTeen, 2008. Information about leading a more environmentally friendly life.

Web Sites

Environmental History Timeline (www .runet.edu/~wkovarik/envhist). A thorough and detailed time line showing important events in the history of the environmental movement.

Environmental News Network (www .enn.com). Articles and links to information regarding the environment. The emphasis is on day-to-day news that concerns the environment.

Environmental Protection Agency (www.epa.gov/history/index.htm). The "History" page provides links and information about the agency's founding and current responsibilities.

Green Guide for Everyday Living (www.thegreenguide.com). Written by environmentalists, this guide describes why and how to cause less environmental destruction.

Greenpeace USA (www.greenpeace .org). Greenpeace is a relatively recent environmental group that tends toward the radical side of the political spectrum. The Web site includes information and links.

Sierra Club (www.sierraclub.org). The Sierra Club was founded by John Muir and others; it is one of many environmental groups currently active today. The Web site provides information about the environment and the history of the club.

Index

Picture Credits

Cover, © Bettman/Corbis

Theodore Chasseriau/The London Art Archive/Alamy, 16

© CountrySideCollection – Homer Sykes/Alamy, 63

Alice Garick/Peter Arnold, Inc./Alamy, 47

© INTERPHOTO/Alamy, 6 (lower)

© North Wind Picture Archives/Alamy, 22, 27, 36

Tom Soucek/Alaska Stock LLC/Alamy, 79

© Wakefield Images/Alamy, 23

XenLights/Alamy, 73

AP Images, 76

Victoria & Albert Museum, London/Art Resource, NY, 17

© Bettmann/Corbis, 7 (lower), 35, 44, 59

© Robert Knudsen/Bettmann/Corbis, 64

© Underwood & Underwood/Bettman/Corbis, 37

© J.L. Kraemer/Blue lantern Studio/Corbis, 6 (upper right)

© Galen Rowell/Documentary Value/Corbis, 39

© Galen Rowell/Encyclopedia/Corbis, 60

© Leonard de Selva/Corbis, 20-21

Bachrach/Hulton Archive/Getty images, 50

FPG/Hulton Archive/Getty Images, 7 (upper left)

J. Wilds/Keystone Features/Hulton Archives/Getty Images, 49

National Archive/Newsmakers/Getty Images, 70

Alfred Eisenstaedt/Time Life Pictures/Getty Images, 51

William Foley/Time Life Picture/Getty Images, 57

Acey Harper/Time Life Pictures/Getty Images, 82

The Library of Congress, 7 (upper right)

National Archives and Records Administration, 6 (upper left)

© North Wind/Nancy Carter/North Wind Picture Archives, 38, 43

© North Wind/North Wind Picture Archives, 13, 14, 29, 31, 33

Image copyright Jostein Hauge, 2009. Used under license from Shutterstock.com, 53

Image copyright Daniel Hebert, 2009. Used under license from Shutterstock.com, 10

Image copyright Jason Maehl, 2009. Used under license from Shutterstock.com, 66

Image copyright Morgan Lane Photography, 2009. Used under license from Shutterstock.com, 75

Image copyright Carolina K. Smith, M.D., 2009. Used under license from Shutterstock.com, 81

About the Author

Stephen Currie has written dozens of books for Lucent and other publishers. He is also a teacher and the author of many educational materials. An enthusiastic hiker, cyclist, and paddler, he has snowshoed in Utah's Wasatch Mountains, kayaked to Death's Door (which is actually in Wisconsin), and climbed New Hampshire's Mount Monadnock in addition to scaling the highest points in six states (an achievement which is less impressive than it sounds). He lives with his family in New York's Hudson River Valley, about 25 miles (40km) upstream from Storm King Mountain.